Genesis
A NEW COMMENTARY

Genesis
A NEW COMMENTARY

Meredith G. Kline

Edited by JONATHAN G. KLINE

HENDRICKSON PUBLISHERS

Genesis: A New Commentary

© 2016 by Hendrickson Publishers Marketing, LLC
P. O. Box 3473
Peabody, Massachusetts 01961-3473
www.hendrickson.com

ISBN 978-1-61970-852-5

All rights reserved. No part of this book may be reproduced or transmitted in any form or by any means, electronic or mechanical, including photocopying, recording, or by any information storage and retrieval system, without permission in writing from the publisher.

All Scripture quotations, unless otherwise indicated, are taken from the Holy Bible, New International Version®, NIV®. Copyright © 1973, 1978, 1984, 2011 by Biblica, Inc.™ Used by permission of Zondervan. All rights reserved worldwide. www.zondervan.com. The "NIV" and "New International Version" are trademarks registered in the United States Patent and Trademark Office by Biblica, Inc.™

Printed in the United States of America

First Printing — November 2016

Cover Photo Credit: ©iStock.com/Igor Zhuravlov
Cover design by Karol Bailey

Library of Congress Cataloging-in-Publication Data

Names: Kline, Meredith G., author.
Title: Genesis : a new commentary / Meredith G. Kline.
Description: Peabody, Massachusetts : Hendrickson Publishers Marketing, 2016.
  | Includes bibliographical references and index.
Identifiers: LCCN 2016028380 | ISBN 9781619708525 (alk. paper)
Subjects: LCSH: Bible. Genesis--Commentaries.
Classification: LCC BS1235.53 .K62 2016 | DDC 222.1107--dc23
  LC record available at https://lccn.loc.gov/2016028380

In loving memory of
Muriel Grace Kline
(1922–2016)

Contents

Foreword	ix
Abbreviations and Cross-Referenced Works	xiii
A Note on the Translation Used	xv
Editor's Preface	xvii

INTRODUCTION
    The Canonical Function of Genesis   1
    The Literary-Thematic Structure of Genesis   2
    Theological Story in Genesis   5
    Authorship   7

PROLOGUE
    Covenant of Creation (1:1–2:3)   9

DIVISION ONE
    City of Man in the Old World (2:4–4:26)   17

DIVISION TWO
    Community of Faith in the Old World (5:1–6:8)   29

DIVISION THREE
    Redemptive Judgment and Re-creation (6:9–9:29)   33

DIVISION FOUR
    City of Man in the New World (10:1–11:9)   45

DIVISION FIVE
    Community of Faith in the New World (11:10–26)   51

DIVISION SIX
    Covenant with Abraham (11:27–25:11)   53

DIVISION SEVEN
    Dismissal from the Covenant (Ishmael) (25:12–18)   89

DIVISION EIGHT
    Isaac, Covenant Patriarch (25:19–35:29)   91

DIVISION NINE
    Dismissal from the Covenant (Esau) (36:1–37:1)   115

DIVISION TEN
    Jacob, Covenant Patriarch (37:2–50:26)   117

Index of Biblical References   143

Foreword

"He's not going to do it again today," I thought to myself on many mornings during Pentateuch class in seminary. One can only tolerate so many paradigm shifts in a month. If I am exaggerating my experience of Dr. Kline's lectures, it is only slightly.

The Gospels are the natural place to find an unfolding narrative of redemption. Many of us began our Christian nurture with John's Gospel. New believers, even non-Christians, can read the Gospel and get the basic plotline of our Lord's incarnation, life, death, and resurrection. And yet the evangelist weaves much of the story around Israel's festivals—landmarks of God's mighty acts in the past—that he presents as fulfilled in Jesus Christ. Old Testament promise and New Testament fulfillment: without knowing something about the former, the latter strikes us gentiles as offering remote and strange details that are incidental to the plot. But they are not incidental, of course; they *are* the plot.

It was from my introduction to Reformed theology that I began to realize that I had been working with only half of the pieces in the puzzle box. Or, to change metaphors, I was walking into an epic film halfway into the story. Of course, I was aware that there were various Old Testament prophecies that Jesus fulfilled. But it was nothing like the libretto of Handel's *Messiah*, where whole chunks of prophetic Scripture were somehow thought to be crucial to Christmas and Easter. In the churches of my youth, it seemed that we did not really know what to do with the Old Testament. Or at least I didn't. Beyond the handful of prophecies we used in apologetics, I assumed that Moses was the paradigmatic lawgiver, that Joshua was the ideal warrior and godly leader, and that the prophets were talking mostly about what would happen in 1948, when Israel became a nation again. One of our hymns, "Dare to Be a Daniel," said it all: these were characters in something closer to Aesop's Fables, with a moral at the end.

I came to Westminster Seminary California convinced that the Old Testament was more than a treasure trove of character studies. But it is one thing to know you should "look for Christ in all of the Scriptures" and quite another to know how to do it and where to find anticipations of Christ from Genesis to Malachi. It was Dr. Kline as well as Mark Futato who provided the other half of those puzzle pieces and, more than that, put them together in such a way that they revealed the figure of Jesus.

This volume is not a commentary in the usual sense. One will not find the author's "homework" in these notes, and originally there were not even any footnotes.[1] It is laconic, concentrating on the key lines in the script. In terms of style, it reads more like a running series of comments—like those in a good study Bible—than a critical engagement with sources, particularly alternative interpretations.

Nevertheless, the homework is there, the fruit of decades of stewing in the juices of the Hebrew text and in the myriad subfields of Old Testament research. After teaching at Westminster Theological Seminary in Philadelphia, Claremont Graduate School, and Reformed Theological Seminary, Kline divided his time in later years between Gordon-Conwell and Westminster Seminary California (1981–2002). All the while, he was an active minister in the Orthodox Presbyterian

---

1. As indicated in the Editor's Preface below, the footnotes in this volume have been added by Dr. Kline's grandson Jonathan.

Church, always committed to preparing ministers to proclaim the whole counsel of God. Dr. Kline's forte was painting a forest without missing the trees. For example, in this work he points out small things in the text, like Hebrew puns on names that highlight the details of the narrative, but he also offers sweeping vistas—more than that, broader categories for interpreting specific details.

First, there is the relationship of canon and covenant, which he had developed especially in *Treaty of the Great King: The Covenantal Structure of Deuteronomy* (1963) and *The Structure of Biblical Authority* (1997). Just as Genesis and the early chapters of Exodus provide a historical prologue to the Sinai covenant, Gen 1–3 is itself a covenantal treaty document in its own right, with a preamble (identifying Yahweh as the Suzerain), a historical prologue (God's lordly rights as Creator of heaven and earth), and the giving of stipulations and sanctions (to Adam as the vassal). The comparison of biblical covenants to Hittite, Assyrian, and Egyptian treaties became a cottage industry in Ancient Near Eastern Studies. But more than any other figure, Dr. Kline, who earned his PhD in Assyriology and Egyptology from Dropsie College, brought these studies into Reformed circles. He brings these insights into fresh explorations of the sacraments in *By Oath Consigned* (1968) and in his remarkable study *Kingdom Prologue: Genesis Foundations for a Covenantal Worldview* (2000), which is a good companion to the present volume.

Second, Dr. Kline highlights the structural divisions within the text itself, particularly the way in which the narrative is arranged according to "the generations of" particular figures. Genealogies are not just random, much less complete sets of, details. The goal is theological: to underscore the dynamic of the covenantal drama in its onward stride toward fulfillment. A further literary division in the patriarchal narratives is created by "the descent of the house of Jacob into

Egypt for their long sojourn in the land of Ham" (p. 117), which in various ways anticipates the career of the greater Jacob and Joseph. Then in Gen 38 all focus turns to Judah's messianic line (p. 120).

Third, and most importantly, Dr. Kline reads the Old Testament in the light of the New, while taking the specifics of the former seriously in their own right. More than typology, his reading focuses on the unfolding plan of redemption in the manner of Geerhardus Vos. The emphasis is not merely on how a person, place, or thing in the Old Testament represents Jesus directly, but on how each episode fits in the developing plotline leading to the Messiah from the promise that God made to Adam and Eve in Gen 3:15. This Christocentric focus is what makes this commentary so personally edifying as well as illuminating. It is God's initiative in sovereign grace that keeps history moving even when the covenant partner seems to bring it all to a standstill by disobedience and unbelief. In other words, Kline connects the dots, as he does in greater detail in other important works, such as *Glory in Our Midst: A Biblical-Theological Reading of Zechariah's Night Visions* (2001) and *God, Heaven and Har Magedon: A Covenantal Tale of Cosmos and Telos* (2006). In addition to his Christocentric focus, his *Images of the Spirit* (1980) provides the richest exploration that I have found concerning the Spirit's person and work in the Old Testament.

It is a singular honor to write the foreword for this posthumously published commentary on Genesis. I trust that you too will discover a treasure of mature wisdom in these pages and, above all, the wonderful truth that Christ himself is the highest wisdom from God.

Michael S. Horton, PhD
J. Gresham Machen Professor of Systematic Theology and Apologetics, Westminster Seminary California

Abbreviations and Cross-Referenced Works

Abbreviations

Heb.	Hebrew
KJV	King James Version
NIV	New International Version

Cross-References

The following books and articles by Meredith G. Kline are referred to in the footnotes of this commentary:

By Oath Consigned: A Reinterpretation of the Covenant Signs of Circumcision and Baptism. Grand Rapids: Eerdmans, 1968.

God, Heaven and Har Magedon: A Covenant Tale of Cosmos and Telos. Eugene, OR: Wipf & Stock, 2006.

Glory in Our Midst: A Biblical-Theological Reading of Zechariah's Night Visions. Overland Park, KS: Two Age Press, 2001.

Images of the Spirit. Grand Rapids: Baker, 1980.

Kingdom Prologue: Genesis Foundations for a Covenantal Worldview. Overland Park, KS: Two Age Press, 2000.

The Structure of Biblical Authority. Grand Rapids: Eerdmans, 1972; 2nd, rev. ed., 1975. [All cross-references to this book in the footnotes of the present work are to the privately published 1989 reprint of the 2nd, rev. ed.]

"Abram's Amen." *Westminster Theological Journal* 31 (1968/69): 1–11.

"Because It Had Not Rained." *Westminster Theological Journal* 20 (1957/58): 146–57.

"Death, Leviathan, and the Martyrs: Isaiah 24:1–27:1." Pp. 229–49 in *A Tribute to Gleason Archer*, ed. Walter C. Kaiser Jr. and Ronald R. Youngblood. Chicago: Moody Press, 1986. Reprinted in *God, Heaven and Har Magedon*, pp. 271–93. [All cross-references to this article in the footnotes of the present work are to the version in *God, Heaven and Har Magedon*.]

"Divine Kingship and Genesis 6:1–4." *Westminster Theological Journal* 24 (1961/62): 187–204.

"The First Resurrection." *Westminster Theological Journal* 37 (1974/75): 366–75.

"The Oracular Origin of the State." Pp. 132–41 in *Biblical and Near Eastern Studies: Essays in Honor of William Sanford LaSor*, ed. Gary A. Tuttle. Grand Rapids: Eerdmans, 1978.

"Space and Time in the Genesis Cosmogony." *Perspectives on Science and the Christian Faith* 48.1 (March 1996): 2–15. Reprinted in *God, Heaven and Har Magedon*, pp. 223–50. [All cross-references to this article in the footnotes of the present work are to the version in *God, Heaven and Har Magedon*.]

"Trial by Ordeal." Pp. 81–93 in *Through Christ's Word: A Festschrift for Dr. Philip E. Hughes*, ed. W. Robert Godfrey and Jesse L. Boyd III. Phillipsburg, NJ: Presbyterian & Reformed, 1985.

A Note on the Translation Used

Unless otherwise marked, the translations of the biblical text in this book are those of the 1984 version of the NIV, though the author has occasionally made slight modifications to this translation without having noted that he has done so.

Editor's Preface

My grandfather wrote the commentary found on the following pages in the mid-1990s, not long after he had finished his magnum opus, *Kingdom Prologue*.[1] The commentary was not published during his lifetime, and it is being made available now for the first time. In 2008, the year after my grandfather passed away, I started going through some boxes containing his old files and came across a typescript of this work tucked away amid his lecture and sermon notes, correspondence from fellow scholars, and various other papers. I proceeded to type the manuscript in electronic format so that it could be better preserved for posterity, but then nearly another decade went by during which, alas, the commentary lay dormant on my hard drive. I am thankful finally to have found the time now to edit the work and prepare it for publication.

Several considerations led me and my colleagues at Hendrickson Publishers, where I presently serve as the academic editor, to name this work (for which my grandfather did not himself provide a title) *Genesis: A New Commentary*. First, as I have mentioned, the commentary, although it is now about twenty years old, is as far as its publication and availability are concerned a new, posthumous piece. The word "new"

---

1. As noted above in the section on Abbreviations and Cross-Referenced Works, the version of *Kingdom Prologue* that is cited in the footnotes of this book was published in 2000, but my grandfather originally published *Kingdom Prologue* privately, in three volumes, from 1981 to 1989.

also seemed appropriate to describe the commentary since, as anyone familiar with my grandfather's other writings or with his teaching is aware (and as Michael Horton's foreword to this book attests), he regularly provided fresh, sometimes paradigm-changing perspectives on how the Bible can be read. Finally, the present commentary is actually the second of two note-style, verse-by-verse commentaries on Genesis that my grandfather wrote; the first appeared in 1970,[2] but—while that one is still interesting and helpful—the present one, which he wrote half a century later, reflects his more mature, developed views on Genesis, especially as he worked them out in the 1980s while he was writing *Kingdom Prologue*.

I have heard students who took my grandfather's course on Old Testament biblical theology, which he taught under various names at several seminaries over the years and which began with a discussion of Gen 1:1, joke that he only rarely made it past Gen 3 by the end of the semester. They would quickly add, however, that in providing a detailed exegesis of these first chapters of the Bible, what he was really doing was taking them on a grand biblical-theological tour covering Genesis to Revelation and all of history—a spiritual and intellectual journey of discovery one can also experience by reading *Kingdom Prologue* (which ostensibly focuses on Gen 1–15) and, to a certain though lesser extent, the present commentary as well. The latter work's nature as a brief, verse-by-verse commentary prodded my grandfather to proffer his perspectives on, if not every verse in the book of Genesis, at least most of them. His penchant for focusing on the book's earlier chapters—which he considered the most theologically significant for the development of redemptive history—still comes through, however: the first two-fifths of the commen-

---

2. "Genesis," in *The New Bible Commentary*, ed. D. Guthrie, 3rd ed. (Downers Grove, IL; InterVarsity Press, 1970), 79–114.

tary is devoted to the so-called primeval history, which constitutes about the first one-fifth of the book of Genesis.

My editorial interventions to this work have been quite minor, though I have done a few things. First, I have performed the normal basic editorial tasks, such as correcting minor errors and making the formatting of the manuscript clear and consistent, and I have also rearranged a small amount of material for clarity. In addition, wherever my grandfather alludes to a Hebrew term, or to more than one (almost invariably with reference to a pun in the text), I have supplied the Hebrew word(s) in question, in transliteration and sometimes with an explanation. My hope is that these additions (which always take the form of footnotes) will clarify certain points that my grandfather makes and provide interested readers with food for further thought or research. Furthermore, to help readers appreciate the fact that, in addition to the new insights it presents, this commentary alludes to or adumbrates a number of sometimes complex positions that my grandfather expanded on in his other writings but could not treat fully in the present context, throughout the commentary I have provided footnotes with cross-references to longer, more nuanced discussions of his ideas found in his other writings.[3] In this way, I hope that this commentary will serve as a starting point for digging deeper into my grandfather's other works, which, as at least one reader has described the process, can—given the headiness of some of his ideas and the sometimes esoteric prose in which he couched them—feel (to shift the metaphor) like drinking from a firehose. Indeed, even though I grew up surrounded by my grandfather's perspectives, I remember

---

3. A number of the articles that are cross-referenced in this commentary will be reprinted by Hendrickson Publishers in 2017 in a volume of my grandfather's collected articles entitled *Essential Writings of Meredith G. Kline*.

what a foreign landscape *Kingdom Prologue* seemed when, as a college student, I read it for the first time—a feeling that was simultaneously thrilling and disorienting. As I worked in the subsequent years to understand my grandfather's ideas more fully, I had the good fortune of sitting down with him in the living room of his home overlooking Beck Pond (a low din of classical radio playing in the background) and asking him for clarification on the framework interpretation or his views on common grace or the millennium. In some ways, his words on the pages that follow, which are pithy and direct, remind me of those face-to-face discussions. My hope is that as you read this commentary, you too will enjoy the experience of having direct access to the thoughts of such an interesting conversation partner, who has helped and, though no longer with us, continues to help us plumb the depths of the word of God.

Jonathan G. Kline, PhD
Associate Editor, Hendrickson Publishers

Genesis: A New Commentary

Introduction

The Canonical Function of Genesis

In biblical times great kings established their rule over lesser kings by covenantal transactions documented in treaties. The Old Testament and New Testament are similar treaty constitutions, or canons, by which the Lord God has governed his people.

The Pentateuch from Exodus on witnesses to the ratification of the Sinaitic covenant (and its renewals under Moses) and presents its commandments along with its offer of blessing and threat of judgment. Preceding such stipulations and sanctions in the international treaties of Moses' day was a declaration of the overlord's claims on the vassal's allegiance, a reminder of his exalted nature and past benefactions. Similarly, Genesis establishes the Lord's claims on the worshipful love of his people by revealing who he is, what he has done, and the covenant of redemption instituted in grace after the fall. Genesis is, then, primarily a revelation of God as Creator-Redeemer and, as such, serves as a treaty preamble and historical prologue to the old covenant canon and indeed to the canonical Scriptures as a whole.

The Literary-Thematic Structure of Genesis

The book of Genesis exhibits the following literary and thematic structure:

Part I
    Prologue: Covenant of Creation (1:1–2:3)

Part II
    Division One: City of Man in the Old World (2:4–4:26)
    Division Two: Community of Faith in the Old World (5:1–6:8)
    Division Three: Redemptive Judgment and Re-creation (6:9–9:29)

Part III
    Division Four: City of Man in the New World (10:1–11:9)
    Division Five: Community of Faith in the New World (11:10–26)
    Division Six: Covenant with Abraham (11:27–25:11)

Part IV
    Division Seven: Dismissal from the Covenant (Ishmael) (25:12–18)
    Division Eight: Isaac, Covenant Patriarch (25:19–35:29)

Part V
    Division Nine: Dismissal from the Covenant (Esau) (36:1–37:1)
    Division Ten: Jacob, Covenant Patriarch (37:2–50:26)

After the revelation of God in the creation prologue as the Maker of all things invisible and visible (1:1–2:3), Genesis is structured in ten divisions, each of which is marked by the superscription formula "This is the account of." This heading is followed by a genealogy of the descendants of the person named therein or by a broader narrative of developments associated with that family. These ten divisions are arranged in two triads followed by two pairs, the whole being integrated with the covenant theme.

The prologue and the first three divisions deal with the world that was (i.e., the period before the flood); the last seven divisions, with the present (i.e., postdiluvian) world. (For this macrostructuring of history, see 2 Pet 3:5–7.) The opening three divisions and the first three of the following seven exhibit a parallel pattern. Both these triads begin with developments in the world of mankind universally (divisions one and four). Next they present a genealogy of the line of redemptive covenant over an extensive period: Adam to Noah through Seth's line (division two) and Shem to Terah (division five). They portray at length epochal covenantal transactions, one with Noah and the other with Abraham (divisions three and six, respectively). The final two pairs expand the record of the Abrahamic Covenant, tracing its confirmation in turn to Isaac and Jacob (divisions eight and ten), in preference to Ishmael and Esau (divisions seven and nine).

This genealogically rooted history of God's covenant, arranged in a repeating pattern of rejection-election, leads to the old and new covenants as successive fulfillments of the kingdom promised to Abraham.

The book of Genesis can be outlined in further detail as follows (the subsections that are listed here under each of the book's divisions constitute the headings in the commentary below):

Prologue: **Covenant of Creation**
(1:1–2:3)
    A. Beginning of heaven and earth (1:1)
      B. Earthly kingdoms (1:2–13)
      B′. Earthly kings (1:14–31)
    A′. King of heaven and earth (2:1–3)

Division One: **City of Man in the Old World**
(2:4–4:26)
    A. Probation in paradise (2:4–25)
    B. Fall and exile curse (3:1–24)
    C. Escalation of evil in the city of man (4:1–24)
    D. Transition: Godly remnant (4:25, 26)

Division Two: **Community of Faith in the Old World**
(5:1–6:8)
    A. Covenant line of Seth (5:1–32)
    B. Transition: Cult of man (6:1–8)

Division Three: **Redemptive Judgment and Re-creation**
(6:9–9:29)
    A. Covenant of salvation with Noah (6:9–8:22)
    B. Common grace covenant (8:20–9:17)
    C. Kingdom oracle (9:18–29)

Division Four: **City of Man in the New World**
(10:1–11:9)
    A. Diaspora of mankind (10:1–32)
    B. Escalation of evil in Babel (11:1–9)

Division Five: **Community of Faith in the New World**
(11:10–26)
    A. Covenant line of Shem (11:10–26)

Division Six: **Covenant with Abraham**
(11:27–25:11)
    A. Introduction: Genealogical sources (11:27–32)
      B. Promised inheritance (12:1–15:20)
        a. Covenant promise and demand (12:1–5)
        b. Difficulties and deliverance (12:6–13:17)
        c. Success and dedication (13:18–14:24)
        d. God's oath of ratification (15:1–20)
    A′. Linkage: Genealogical resources (16:1–16)
      B′. Promised heir (17:1–22:19)
        a. Covenant promise and demand (17:1–37)
        b. Difficulties and deliverance (18:1–19:38)
        c. Success and dedication (20:1–21:34)
        d. God's oath of confirmation (22:1–19)
    A″. Conclusion: Genealogical succession
        (22:20–25:11)

Division Seven: **Dismissal from the Covenant**
(25:12–18)
    A. Rejected line of Ishmael (25:12–18)

Introduction

Division Eight: **Isaac, Covenant Patriarch**
(25:19–35:29)
    A. Jacob's election as successor (25:19–27:40)
        a. Jacob's struggle for the birthright (25:19–34)
        b. Blessings for Isaac in Canaan (26:1–33)
        c. Jacob's reception of Isaac's blessing (26:34–27:40)
    B. Exile origin of the tribal fathers (27:41–33:17)
        a. Jacob's flight from the land (27:41–28:9)
        b. Encounter with God's angel at Bethel (28:10–22)
        c. Conflict with Laban (29:1–30)
        d. Birth of Jacob's sons (29:31–30:24)
        c′. Pact with Laban (30:25–31:55)
        b′. Encounter with God's angel at Peniel (32:1–32)
        a′. Jacob's return to the land (33:1–17)
    C. Israel in Canaan under Isaac (33:18–35:29)

Division Nine: **Dismissal from the Covenant**
(36:1–37:1)
    A. Rejected line of Esau (36:1–37:1)

Division Ten: **Jacob, Covenant Patriarch**
(37:2–50:26)
    A. Family disunion in Canaan (37:2–38:30)
        B. Joseph in Egypt (39:1–41:57)
            C. Refining of the covenant family (42:1–45:28)
        B′. Jacob's family in Egypt (46:1–47:27)
    A′. Reunion and restoration to Canaan (47:28–50:26)

THEOLOGICAL STORY IN GENESIS

In setting the law in its historical context, Genesis concentrates on the Abrahamic Covenant (Gen 12–50), for the Mosaic order was a fulfillment of its specific kingdom promises. Since that covenant stood in continuity with previous redemptive covenant, which itself resumed the kingdom objectives of the creation covenant, Genesis includes a review of these foundational beginnings (Gen 1–11). Creation, fall, and redemption with its prospect of consummation—that is the basic outline of the theological story. Genesis tells of the Creator-Lord who, in spite of the devil's opposition and man's revolt against heaven, directs earthly history and guides his covenant people toward the perfecting of his kingdom.

In Gen 3–8, the pattern of redemption unfolds in a complete world history. The rest of Genesis depicts redemption in the postdiluvian world, particularly as shaped by the Abrahamic Covenant. Though the patriarchal community is traced only through its pilgrim stage, when the outward establishment of the kingdom through divine judgment on Canaan was still abeyant, what stands out is the sovereignty of the divine purpose and the omnipotence of the Redeemer-Lord. The irresistible process of election; the miraculous origination of the promised seed and their supernatural, spiritual transformation; the remarkable preservation of the covenant family amid the world powers—the entire history proclaims God's absolute authority and total control over nature and nations in the furtherance of his redemptive purpose, an earnest of his later fulfillment of the kingdom promises through Moses and Christ.

By this focus on redemption, Genesis points to Christ, in and through whom redemption attains its goal. The genealogical framework itself is oriented to the promised messianic king. For royal genealogies functioned in the ancient world to legitimate throne claims, and similarly the overall genealogical records of Scripture are designed to trace back to royal grants (cf. Gen 1:27, 28; 17:6; 49:10) the lineage of king David (see 1 Chr 2 and 3; cf. 5:1; 9:1) and "Jesus Christ, the son of David, the son of Abraham" (Matt 1:1). Christ is also heralded in Genesis by prophetic words and typological figures and events. Indeed, he appears himself there in the Angel of the Lord, judge of the wicked and deliverer of the patriarchs in their earthly pilgrimage to God's heavenly city.

Authorship

The Law (or Pentateuch) is attributed to Moses consistently in the Old Testament and was regarded as Mosaic by the Jews, a judgment endorsed by Jesus and his inspired New Testament spokesmen (cf. esp. John 1:45; 5:46f.). The Book of Genesis lacks within itself the more explicit claims to Mosaic authorship naturally present in the other Pentateuchal books, which deal with Moses' own times and his mediatorship of the old covenant. However, not only was Genesis part of the Law viewed as Mosaic by Jesus, but its own contents identify it as manifestly a prologue to Exodus–Deuteronomy. Genesis presents the covenant with the fathers whose promises God "remembers" in his exodus acts and Sinai covenant making. It provides the identification of the nation of Israel, the subject from Exodus on. In fact, the genealogical record of Israel's roots continues from Genesis into Exodus (cf. Gen 46:8ff.; Exod 1:1ff.; 6:14ff.). Numerous other thematic strands interlock Genesis with the rest of the Pentateuch, and in their own way even the discredited modern theories alleging multiple strands running from Genesis through Numbers attest to the literary continuity of Genesis with the following books. As noted, the canonical function of Genesis is that of treaty preamble and historical prologue to the Mosaic covenant. Certainly these foundations do not come from a later time than the superstructure, but were composed by Moses as the necessary introduction to his five-book work.

PROLOGUE

COVENANT OF CREATION
(1:1–2:3)

A prologue on creation opens the Genesis history of God's kingdom, revealing him as the One of whom and unto whom are all things.

BEGINNING OF HEAVEN AND EARTH
(1:1)

1:1 ▷ **In the beginning.** Proverbs 8:22, 23 interprets this as a time before the developments recounted in vv. 2ff., not their earliest stage, nor yet the entire creation week. It extends from the absolute beginning of the space-time world to the point where "earth" existed in the embryonic form described in v. 2. From that "earth" the visible heavens were derived (see note on vv. 6–8). Hence the "heaven" distinguished from it in the prior "beginning" time (v. 1) is the invisible heavens of God's Glory and angels, a realm created complete with its hosts at this "beginning." God stands at the beginning of Scripture, the Eternal and there is none else (cf. Isa 40:21, 28; 43:10), Creator of everything visible and invisible (Col 1:17; John 1:1). This truth is the foundation of all knowledge.

Earthly Kingdoms
(1:2–13)

1:2–5 ▷ Earth (v. 2): the visible world, to be transformed from inchoate planet (cf. Deut 32:10), lightless and landless, into a paradisaic dwelling (Isa 45:18; cf. Prov 8:30ff.). Days one to three describe the bounding of darkness and deep. Earth is structured into three realms: day-and-night; the seas, separated from the firmament of clouds; and dry land, above the waters and vivified by them. Days four to six relate the filling of these realms with the hosts of heaven, sea, and earth.

Spirit of God (v. 2). Hovering eagle-like (cf. Deut 32:11) aloft in the invisible heavens was the Architect of creation, his Glory filling, indeed constituting, the celestial temple. This Glory, manifested on earth as the Shekinah-cloud, is called the Spirit (see Neh 9:19, 20; Isa 63:11–14; Hag 2:5). Here was the omniscience and omnipotence to turn dark deep into cosmic house of God (cf. Isa 66:1) and habitat for man, to bring the infinite construction to Sabbath consummation.

God said (v. 3). God created by sovereign fiat, without tools and without preexisting materials (cf. Heb 11:3; John 1:3; Pss 33:6, 9; 148:5).

Light (v. 3). This is identified in v. 5 as the day-light that alternates with night on earth. According to vv. 14–18, it is an effect produced by the sun, whose existence is assumed here (an indication that the narrative sequence is not designed to correspond to the chronological sequence of creation history).[1] The initial appearance of light in the universe and the forming of the sun and stars transpired in the "beginning" time (v. 1).

Good (v. 4) signifies a result that furthers the architectural goal of a habitable earth. Even the darkness, now called

---

1. "Space and Time in the Genesis Cosmogony," 236–40, 249; "Because It Had Not Rained," esp. 146, 152–54, 156–57.

"night" and bounded by the day, serves earthlings usefully (Ps 104:20–23).

God called (v. 5). Creative fiat, "let there be," was accompanied repeatedly by authoritative naming. Existence and meaning thus were given together as the Creator executed his eternal counsel. The world comes into existence fully interpreted, with no mysteries for its Maker, though for man the divine wisdom in creation be unfathomable and the Creator himself beyond comprehension (cf. Job 28 and 38). Hence, the beginning of wisdom for man is the fear of the Lord (Job 28:38).

First day (v. 5). The relevant biblical evidence indicates that the image of a week of days with their evenings and mornings is a literary figure not to be taken literally (see notes on 1:14–18; 2:2 and 5).[2]

1:6–8 ▷ The restructuring of the dark, dead deep into a watering system of rain clouds, springs, and rivers supportive of life is dealt with under days two and three. In the formation of earth's atmosphere, the waters above—i.e., the clouds (cf. Prov 8:28)—were separated from the seas below. This also resulted in the canopy-like expanse called "sky." The "sky" and the clouds constitute the visible heavens, the first and second heaven respectively in biblical terminology. The atmosphere was also essential to the day-light mentioned under day one.

1:9–13 ▷ The emergence of the **dry ground** (v. 9) sets bounds on the waters below (cf. Job 38:8–11). Vegetation, a subordinate life-form, was introduced into the land realm to serve the higher forms of land-based life (cf. Gen 1:29, 30).

According to their kinds (v. 12). The creation "week" was a definite closed period within which God produced all the significant varieties of life-forms he had planned. There is no

---

2. "Space and Time in the Genesis Cosmogony," esp. 223, 243–44, 250; "Because It Had Not Rained," esp. 154–57.

cosmic principle of evolution at work on its own, outside the bounds of the creation "week," producing new "kinds."

EARTHLY KINGS
(1:14–31)

1:14–19 ▷ The accomplishments described under days one and four are the same: daylight appears on earth and is separated from the darkness, so forming the cycle of day and night. This repetition of the creative event of day one in day four shows the narrative is not arranged in chronological order but thematically.[3]

Made two great lights . . . stars (v. 16). The creation of the starry hosts had been in process from the beginning.

Govern (vv. 16, 18). The theme of days four to six is the appointment of rulers over the realms of days one to three. Thus, the sun and moon would regulate their domain, the day-night cycle (cf. Ps 136:7–9). However, the astral bodies are not divine rulers, as in pagan mythology, but creatures of God, serving man with illumination and calendar signs (cf. Ps 104:19–23).

1:20–23 ▷ The **birds** of the heaven (v. 20; cf. vv. 26, 28, 30) and the creatures of the sea were given the realms of day two (the parallel to day five), the sky above and the waters below.

God blessed them (v. 22). Their dominion was that of occupying their realm through multiplication, for which they were empowered by the creative blessing of fecundity. This was a nature parable of the kingship of man, to whom a similar blessing-commission was given (1:28; cf. 2:3; 5:2).

---

3. "Space and Time in the Genesis Cosmogony," 236–40, 249; "Because It Had Not Rained," esp. 146, 152–54, 156–57.

God created (v. 21). The original verb of creation[4] in v. 1 is used again with the first mention of living creatures, those animated by the breath of life (v. 20; cf. 1:24, 30; 9:10, 16).

1:24, 25 ▷ Like day three, day six includes two divine works: animals (vv. 24, 25) and man (vv. 26–28). Given dominion over the land-realm of day three, the animals would receive its produce as tribute (cf. v. 30).

1:26–31 ▷ **Let us make** (v. 26). God's creative fiat was addressed to the angels of his heavenly temple-court (cf. 3:22, 24; 11:7; 18:2, 21; Isa 6:8), the Spirit-temple (see note on 1:2). This Glory-Spirit was the Archetype for the creation of man.[5] Made in the likeness of this holy Lord of Glory, man was invested with dominion (like the angels, cf. Ps 8:5), moral excellence (cf. Eph 4:24; Gal 3:10), and the prospect of glorification (cf. 1 Cor 15:49ff.).

Male and female (v. 27). Each is individually the image of God, apart from their relationship.

Fill the earth and subdue it (v. 28). Man's creation was a coronation. In both fiat (v. 26) and fulfillment (vv. 27, 28), his likeness to God is linked to his royalty (cf. 3:22; 9:6). He was made lord over the animal (v. 28) and plant (v. 29) kingdoms. Vegetation was not the total provision of food for man; animals were also fair game (cf. 1 Tim 4:3–5; 2 Pet 2:12). Specific mention of plants as food prepares for the special prohibition of the tree of knowledge (2:16, 17). Reaching beyond the land realm, man's dominion included all the realms of days one to three and all the rulers of days four to six. His historical mission was to extend the kingdom of God from its cultic focus

---

4. Heb. *b-r-ʾ*.
5. *Images of the Spirit*, 13–34, esp. 21–24, 26–34; *Kingdom Prologue*, 32, 42–46; *God, Heaven and Har Magedon*, 33, 36–37; "Space and Time in the Genesis Cosmogony," 233.

at the mountain of God in Eden (see notes on 2:8–14) to the fullness of a global city of God.[6] Through procreation, blessed by God, the original couple would people the planet. Royal labor, in imitation of the Creator-King and prospered by him, would bring the earth increasingly into man's service until the mandated cultural task was completed.

All . . . very good (v. 31). This anticipates God's Sabbath delight in the perfect execution of his architectural design (cf. Prov 8:30ff.).

King of Heaven and Earth (2:1–3)

2:1–3 ▷ Verse 1 summarizes the creation of the invisible and visible worlds with all their occupants (cf. Neh 9:6).

He rested (v. 2): another, loftier coronation scene (see note on 1:28). God's Sabbath resting is a royal session on the heavenly throne of his cosmic temple-palace (cf. Isa 66:1). It celebrates the completion of creation and reveals that God, the Alpha, is also the Omega.[7] This Sabbath reign knows no ending. Thus, the seventh day has no evening-morning formula; it continues forever and believers are invited to participate in it at last (Heb 4:3–10). Here is a further indication of the figurative nature of the seven-day scheme of the creation prologue.[8]

Made it holy (v. 3). As the Exod 20:11 quotation of Gen 2:3 shows, the subject changes in this verse from God's seventh day (v. 2) to the ordinance of the Sabbath appointed for man's

---

6. *Kingdom Prologue*, 68–70; *God, Heaven and Har Magedon*, 47.

7. *Kingdom Prologue*, 33–41; *God, Heaven and Har Magedon*, 61; "Space and Time in the Genesis Cosmogony," 241.

8. "Space and Time in the Genesis Cosmogony," 241–42; "Because It Had Not Rained," 154–57.

observance. The latter was a sign of God's covenant, promising ultimate entrance into the glorified state, the perfecting of God's glory-image in man, and the culmination of man's historical mission of building God's kingdom-temple. It summoned man to imitate the Sabbath pattern set by his divine Archetype and so confess God as Author and Finisher and himself as image-son. It called man to celebration of God's triumphant lordship and consecration of himself and his kingdom achievements to him "of whom and unto whom are all things" (Rom 11:36).

DIVISION ONE

City of Man in the Old World (2:4–4:26)

Probation in Paradise (2:4–25)

2:4 ▷ **This is the account.** This heading marks the division of Genesis after the creation prologue into ten parts. All of v. 4 forms a unit (as the resultant chiasm confirms), an expanded version of the superscription formula (cf. Num 3:1). Here, as everywhere else, the heading refers not to antecedents or ancestry but to descendants or developments in the family of the party named. Hence it identifies this section (Gen 2:4–4:26) not as a second account of the origin of heaven and earth but as the sequel to creation.

The Lord God. This combination of the term God and the proper name Yahweh ("Lord" in NIV) appears as often in 2:4–3:24 as in the rest of the Old Testament. It identifies Israel's covenant Lord, Yahweh, as the Alpha-Omega God of the creation prologue.

2:5–25 ▷ The focus narrows in 1:2 to the visible world, the earth, and here in 2:5 to man's original locale, Eden, as the stage is set for the covenant crisis of Gen 3. The man and woman, the principals, are reintroduced (cf. 1:27) at the beginning (vv. 5–7) and end (vv. 18–25). In between are accounts of the garden, site of the climactic probation test (vv. 8–14), and the critical stipulation of the covenant (vv. 15–17). God's covenants were legal transactions with divinely sanctioned commitments, instruments of the divine government.[1] Covenants offering God's kingdom of life as their blessing-sanction have stipulations. The consummated kingdom is a grant awarded for faithful service. Under the Covenant of Creation the first Adam was to have rendered this, but it was actually performed by the second Adam under redemptive covenant.

2:5–7 ▷ Because of the crucial role of the two special trees (mentioned in 2:9), the narrative relates the origin of man to that of plant life.

No plant (v. 5). At some point within the creation "week," God had not introduced plant life because there was no rain for the fields and no man to irrigate the agricultural land. Genesis 2 thus assumes natural providential preservation of vegetation during the creation era, which would be contradicted by Genesis 1 if interpreted as a literal, sequential narrative with vegetation present on day three, before the creation of the sun on day four.[2] Streams issuing from the earth remedied the absence of water (v. 6) and then man the agriculturalist was made (v. 7).

God . . . breathed (v. 7): an anthropomorphism for the fathering agency of the Spirit (cf. John 20:22; Ezek 37:1–10, 14).

Man from . . . ground (v. 7). The Hebrew wordplay is reflected in Paul's commentary that the first Adam was fashioned in a natural body for earthly existence. The apostle fur-

---

1. *Kingdom Prologue*, 1–6.
2. "Space and Time in the Genesis Cosmogony," 223–24, 243–50; "Because It Had Not Rained."

ther observed that the last Adam shared in the earthy state in order to secure for fallen man in the resurrection the spiritual body of imperishable glory (1 Cor 15:42–49), the prospect forfeited by the first Adam.

2:8–14 ▷ Man's homeland, somewhere in the Near East (v. 14), being provisioned with all the satisfactions of earthly life, pressed upon man the claims of his Sovereign's lovingkindness for a response of loving obedience and service. In the center of the garden (and in the literary center of Gen 2) were the two special trees (v. 9), key elements in man's probation. These religious symbols indicate that paradise was a sanctuary, the garden of God (Isa 51:3; Ezek 28:13; 31:8ff.), the cultic center of the earth. Here was the mountain of God, crowned by the Glory with cherubim retinue (cf. Ezek 28:13ff.; Gen 3:24), the source of the life-giving river that watered the encompassing lands (cf. Rev 22:1, 2; Ezek 47:1).

The tree of life (v. 9), fructified by that river, symbolically promised and would seal glorified eternal life as the reward of successful probation (cf. Rev 22:14; Gen 3:22).

2:15–17 ▷ Man's covenant obligations, both royal-cultural and priestly-cultic, are summarized in v. 15. Making the earth serve man (cf. 1:28) meant man must serve, or cultivate, it (NIV, "work it"). Because the garden was holy, man must guard it (NIV, "take care of it"). The latter verb[3] is a common term for the priests' function of protecting God's sanctuary from defiling encroachment (cf. 3:24).

The knowledge of good and evil (v. 17) is judicial discernment (cf. 2 Sam 14:17; 1 Kgs 3:9, 28). The tree of that name pointed to Adam's priestly task of judging the evil one when he intruded into God's holy garden.

---

3. Heb. *š-m-r*.

You must not eat (v. 17). The focal probationary proscription was an exception to man's dominion (cf. 1:29). While the tree of knowledge exalted Adam over Satan, it confronted him with the Creator's sovereignty over him.[4]

Surely die (v. 17). A curse balanced the covenant's promised blessing, symbolized by the tree of life and Sabbath, threatening the opposite—not physical death but eternal perdition (later called "second death").[5]

2:18–25 ▷ **A helper suitable** (v. 18). Peopling the earth required that the man be joined by the woman, his helper (cf. 1 Cor 11:9) and, unlike any previously existing earthling (vv. 19, 20), man's likeness (cf. 1 Cor 11:7), like him the image of God (cf. 1:28).

The man gave names (v. 20). In imitation of God (cf. 1:5, 8, etc.), man engaged in the authoritative process of assigning names.

A woman from the rib (v. 22). The apostle Paul's comment (1 Cor 11:8) disallows figurative interpretation, and such an origin of the first female of the species precludes the theory of an evolutionary emergence of humans through a prior life-continuum. Eve's derivation from her husband involved her institutional subordination to his authority (1 Cor 11:3). Her likeness-derivation thus affords an analogy to man (generically) as image of God under his Author's authority (cf. 1 Cor 11:7).

Be united to (v. 24), or cleave to, is a term for covenantal commitment. Marriage provides a societal parable of God's covenant with man as a troth engagement. It was the community structure in which the covenant theocracy was embodied on earth at the first.[6]

---

4. *Kingdom Prologue*, 103–7.
5. *Kingdom Prologue*, 101–3; "The First Resurrection," 367, 371, 373–74.
6. *Kingdom Prologue*, 70–74.

Fall and Exile Curse
(3:1–24)

3:1–6 ▷ The creation order was a covenant of works, i.e., justification and attainment of the Sabbath-kingdom would be the reward for meritorious achievement in a probation event. God confronted Adam, priestly guardian of the sanctuary, with Satan, a hostile intruder, to be overcome and rebuked in God's name. This victory would be the critical act of righteousness, involving also obedience to the special probationary prohibition (cf. 2:17).

Crafty (v. 1). Satan's serpentine embodiment matched his sinuously deceptive encroachment and temptation (cf. Rev 12:9). Challenge to God's prohibition (v. 1) and contradiction of God's threat (vv. 4, 5) betrayed the anti-lord identity of the deceiver-usurper.

She . . . ate it (v. 6). The woman revolted against the covenant of the Lord of life and light and sealed an alliance with the rival prince of death and darkness.[7]

Gave some to her husband (v. 6). In approaching the woman and ignoring the man's prior responsibility, Satan had subverted God's marriage ordinance. The woman had not questioned that and now radically repudiated the marriage covenant with her husband, while breaking the covenant with her God.[8]

He ate (v. 6). Faced with seduction to idolatry, he should have condemned his wife (cf. Deut 13:6ff.) and expelled the idol-lord. Because he was by God's appointment representative of all mankind in this probation, condemnation and death came upon all by this sin of the one (Rom 5:12–19).[9]

---

7. *Kingdom Prologue*, 122–27.
8. *Kingdom Prologue*, 129–30.
9. *Kingdom Prologue*, 127.

3:7–13 ▷ **Naked** (v. 7). Intimacy appropriate within marriage (2:25) brought a sense of shame in their state of virtual divorce. In Hebrew, "naked" puns on "crafty" (v. 1):[10] sin had turned them into the image of the devil. The Lord's advent was "as the Spirit of the (judgment) day" (v. 8, literally), i.e., in the terrifying Glory-Spirit theophany, heralded by thunder-trumpet (cf. Sinai and note on 1:2).[11]

They hid (v. 8), guilty of breaking their covenant union with God and conscious of spiritual nakedness through loss of their ethical likeness to God. A preliminary judicial interrogation evoked Satan-like distortions of truth and malicious accusations, even recriminations against God (vv. 9–13). All efforts to conceal their sin succeeded only in exposing it.[12]

3:14, 15 ▷ Intimations of salvation accompanied the announcement of Satan's damnation.

Cursed are you (v. 14). Using the serpentine imagery of Satan's chosen medium of approach, the heavenly Judge declared his punishment, ultimate in degree and perpetual in duration—though delayed in its execution to make historical space for the program of reconciliation prophesied in v. 15.

I will put enmity (v. 15). Renewal of covenant with God was expressed by its negative corollary, alienation from Satan. By sovereign divine initiative, reconciliation would be effected between God and a new humanity, elect in the messianic descendant of the woman (cf. Rom 16:20; Rev 12). Satan's **offspring** are reprobate men (cf. John 8:33, 34; 1 John 3:8ff.).

He ... you (v. 15). In the decisive battle, the two armies are represented by individual champions, Christ and Satan.

---

10. Heb. ʿērōm, "naked" (3:7); ʿārûm, "crafty" (3:1).
11. *Kingdom Prologue*, 128–29; *Images of the Spirit*, 97–131.
12. *Kingdom Prologue*, 129–31.

Head ... heel (v. 15). Christ will execute the curse on Satan here announced. Victory over the Adversary, bringing deliverance to the rest of the woman's seed, involves atonement for sin. Suffering is the way to Messiah's glory (Isa 53:12; Luke 24:26, 46; 1 Pet 1:11; Rev 12:10, 11).

3:16–19 ▷ During the interim, until the final judgment on Satan and his seed and the consummation of the redemption of God's elect, all fallen mankind would be under a common curse, temporal and tempered by God's common grace.[13]

Rule over you (v. 16). In the fall, the marriage institution had been violated and, though continued and in measure blessed with children, it would be beset with difficulties in the procreation process. Also, the husband's rightful authority would become a tyrannical mastery over a wife trying to dominate him (cf. Gen 4:7 for the idiom).

Cursed is the ground (v. 17) **... return to the ground** (v. 19). Man's transgression had involved the realm of nature, and the task of subduing it, though successful in measure by God's common grace, would be a frustrating, painful process culminating in death. Cursing the ground did not introduce new objects or laws of nature. The curse consisted in the earth's dominating and victimizing royal man, even reclaiming him. Recoiling from this Sheol-function under the common curse, earth groans, longing for its resurrection deliverance (Rom 8:20ff.).[14]

Dust you are (v. 19). Man's being made with an earthy body did not make physical death inevitable, but possible, as a consequence of sin.

3:20, 21 ▷ **Named his wife Eve ... living** (v. 20). Adam thus responded in faith to the mother promise of v. 15.

---

13. *Kingdom Prologue*, 153–55.
14. "Death, Leviathan, and the Martyrs," esp. 276–80.

Clothed them (v. 21). Spreading a garment over another was a pledging of troth (cf. Ruth 3:9). The Lord symbolically sealed his promise to renew his (marriage) covenant with the woman and her seed (cf. v. 15), and by the same token reunited Adam and Eve in their earthly marriage.

Garments of skin. A sacrificed animal provided the covering-remedy for the nakedness of divorce, symbolic of the atoning suffering of the woman's messianic seed.

3:22–24 ▷ Banished him (v. 23). The judgment scene concludes with a cleansing of the temple. The Lord had expelled Satan, the mission man failed to perform. But fallen mankind, represented in Adam and Eve, was now defiled and must also be banished from the holy garden (cf. Rev 21:27). The interim world is an exile existence in a wilderness under the shadow of death.

Cherubim . . . a flaming sword (v. 24). Angels regularly attend God's advent in Glory for judgment (cf. 3:8). They took over man's forfeited guardianship of Eden (cf. 3:15), preventing access until the Son of Man, when slaying the dragon-accuser, vicariously suffered the sword of judgment on the tree of death and so reopened the way to the tree of life.

ESCALATION OF EVIL IN THE CITY OF MAN (4:1–24)

4:1, 2 ▷ Cain . . . Abel. The prophesied division of mankind into two spiritually opposed groups (cf. 3:15) took place at once. This section (2:4–4:26) traces the escalation of sin in the ungodly line of Cain through the generations leading to the flood.

Flocks . . . soil. Exiled from Eden, mankind by God's common grace still enjoyed a degree of dominion over the earth and its creatures. Bible-honoring reconstructions of the history of human culture must reckon with the presence of food production and animal husbandry from earliest prediluvian times.

4:3–8 ▷ Cain betrayed his kinship to the devil by his enmity against the woman's righteous seed (cf. 1 John 3:12).

An offering (v. 3). Token consecratory sacrifices would have been appropriate even in sinless worship. Cain's hatred erupted at the altar. This was not social-economic but religious strife.

Favor on Abel (v. 4). In contrast to Cain, Abel offered in faith and love—witness his selection of the choicest for the Lord (cf. Heb 11:4). Divine acceptance was probably by special sign (cf. Lev 9:24; Judg 6:21); certainly special word revelation continued in the covenant community.

Sin is crouching (v. 7). God's warning pictures Cain's murderous purpose like an entrance-demon (an allusion to serpent-Satan) coiled at the door of his heart, desiring to master him. Jesus echoed this warning to those who schemed to kill him (John 8:37), exposing them as children of the devil, the murderer from the beginning, whose desire they were bent on carrying out (John 8:44).

Killed him (v. 8). Divine warning no more deterred Cain from spilling the first martyr blood than it did those later children of the serpent through whose agency the devil struck the heel of the woman's messianic seed.

4:9–15 ▷ **I don't know** (v. 9). In reply to God's judicial inquiry, Cain, like Adam and Eve, was evasive and mendacious, so displaying further his likeness to the devil, father of lies (John 8:44).

Your brother's blood (v. 10). Cain could not hide his blood sacrifice to the devil in the ground any more than Adam and Eve could hide from God in the shadows. The cry of martyr Abel's blood was heard in heaven (cf. Matt 23:35; Rev 6:10; Isa 26:21), as would be that of Christ, which called for pardon rather than vengeance (cf. Heb 12:24), though it too required vindication.

Cursed are you (v. 11). God identified Cain with Satan in cursedness (cf. 3:14), though this curse was not yet the doom of hell but an aggravation of the common curse on fallen mankind previously announced to Adam and Eve (cf. 3:16–19). On that earlier occasion, after the fall, the family was reinstituted; here the common grace institution of the state is promulgated.[15]

Hidden from your presence (v. 14). Cain feared his fugitive existence would be in a world beyond God's judicial oversight, without a law order to deter vendetta against him.

Vengeance seven times over (v. 15). Sevenfold signifies a divine judicial order. Here is the divine charter for the city as wielder of the sword of justice, an arrangement whose implementation is immediately noted (see v. 17). Gen 9:5, 6 records the postdiluvian resumption of the state. In v. 15b, God's disclosure to Cain is described as an oath (mistranslated "mark"), declaring that the absolute anarchy he feared would not obtain.

4:17–24 ▷ **City** (v. 17). Though legitimated by God's appointment, founding of the city of man was ominous because of the antichrist spirit of the founder, a saint-slayer.

Named it after his son (v. 17). The perverse direction mankind would give to the state, turning it into a bestial, self-idolizing power, was foreshadowed in Cain's dedication of it to his own dynastic fame. The brief history of developing urban culture in the line of Cain (vv. 17–22) underscores the

---

15. On this and the following two paragraphs, see "The Oracular Origin of the State."

commonness of the common grace gifts like institutions and inventive genius, which are bestowed on the wicked as well as the righteous.

Lamech (v. 19). Evil in the dynasty of Cain culminated in a royal tyrant who abused the marriage institution by practicing bigamy (v. 19) and used the state, the institution for justice (life for life), to perpetrate gross injustice (life for wound) for personal vengeance (v. 23). Here was legalized murder, a situation worse than the anarchical feuding Cain feared.

Seventy-seven times (v. 24). This boast of king Lamech alludes to the original city charter (cf. v. 15), which he repudiated, asserting his own autonomy, indeed his own superiority to the God of mere sevenfold judgment. Sin in the line of the serpent's seed here reached the antichrist stage as man assumed the name of super-god. This theme is resumed in Gen 6:4.[16]

Transition: Godly Remnant (4:25, 26)

4:25, 26 ▷ A transition is made here from the line of Cain, the subject of this section of Genesis, to the theme of the elect line dealt with in the next section.

Seth (v. 25). His name expressed Eve's faith that God would continue the covenant line until the mother promise was fulfilled.

Call on the name of the LORD (v. 26). This idiom is used for adopting a surname in recognition of a forebear. In contrast to the Cainites' passion for the name of man, a remnant community raised the banner of God's name, confessing the Lord as their Father and Protector.

---

16. "The Oracular Origin of the State," 137; "Divine Kingship and Genesis 6:1–4," esp. 195–96, 201; *Kingdom Prologue*, 183–87.

DIVISION TWO

COMMUNITY OF FAITH IN THE OLD WORLD (5:1–6:8)

COVENANT LINE OF SETH (5:1–32)

5:1 ▷ The tenfold heading of Genesis appears here in the modified form reflected in Matt 1:1. Having followed prediluvian history to a climax of evil in Cain's line, the narrative returns to Adam and treats the same epoch from the perspective of the line that called on the name of the Lord (cf. 4:26). The history is cast in the form of a genealogy, appropriate to the story of the covenant community, which was embodied in the family institution. The genealogy is selective, not exhaustive. This is signalized by the conventional numbers: ten generations from Adam to Noah, with three sons of Noah, paralleled in the genealogy of the covenant line in 11:10–26 by the ten generations from Shem to Terah and his three sons. (Cf. Matt 1, where the clearly incomplete genealogy is composed of three sets of double sevens.) Hence the age figures of these patriarchs cannot be used to compute chronologies.

5:2–32 ▷ **Son ... image** (v. 3). By the juxtaposing of the statements that Adam fathered a son in his image-likeness and that God created humans in his image (v. 2), the image of God is explained by sonship and so identified as a matter of representational likeness, not of representative office, though that too is involved. The fact of life spans upward of a millennium is reflected in greatly exaggerated form in Mesopotamian traditions, especially concerning prediluvian kings.

Then he died (vv. 5, 8, 14, etc.). This refrain attests the fulfillment of the dust-unto-dust curse (cf. 3:19). Its use to punctuate the genealogy of the godly line points up the truth that through the one man Adam and his sin, death had come as a common curse upon all men, wicked or righteous (cf. Rom 5:12–14). However, the main purpose of this genealogy is to witness to the Lord's faithfulness in preserving the messianic line in the fallen world in the face of Satan's enmity manifested in the escalation of the anti-God spirit of the world rulers. All true faith was not necessarily restricted to Seth's descendants all this time, and certainly not all Sethites worshipped the Lord, but in the Sethite line the covenant community found continuous representation from Adam to Noah's day. Indeed, by then it was restricted to the Noahic family of the Sethites. Its reduction to so small a remnant suggests the fierceness of satanic persecution from without and the subtlety of his deception within. To address warnings to the apostates from within and the ungodly without, God raised up prophets among his people, like Enoch (vv. 21–24; cf. Jude 14, 15) and Noah (2 Pet 2:5). Each of these **walked with God** (vv. 22, 24; cf. 6:9), that is, they received special revelation, caught up in the Spirit, and were associated with the Lord in his judicial confrontation with mankind (cf. the use of this verb in Gen 3:8; Job 1:7; 22:14; Zech 1:11).

God took him (v. 24). The prophets Enoch and Elijah introduced warning stages in God's covenant lawsuit in their respective ages, and these two alone of mankind were translated directly to heaven (cf. Heb 11:5), a prophetic sign—in the midst of prevailing death (vv. 5, 8, etc.)—of the redemptive victory over the prince of death to be won by the coming Messiah (cf. Pss 49:15 [Heb. 16]; 73:24).

Noah . . . comfort (v. 29): a wordplay.[1] In stark contrast to the blasphemous boast of Cainite Lamech (cf. 4:24), Sethite Lamech's naming of the son by whom God would preserve the faithful remnant expressed a longing for the heavenly realm to which God took Enoch, beyond this sin-cursed temporal existence.

Transition: Cult of Man (6:1–8)

6:1–8 ▷ Again, a major division of Genesis closes with a transitional section (cf. 4:25, 26). In preparation for the judgment theme that follows, Gen 6:1–7 shifts back from the preceding focus on the godly line to take up again ominous developments in the city of man (cf. Gen 4:17–24). The climax of mankind's revolt against God reached in Cainite Lamech's reign is here portrayed again, with its consequences.[2]

Sons of God (v. 2), or sons of the gods. Precisely the same three types of offenses committed by King Lamech are attributed to these figures: (1) *Abuse of marriage.* They collected in their royal harems "all that they chose" (v. 2). (2) *Perverting the state into an agency of injustice.* They filled the earth with violence (cf. vv. 5, 11). (3) *Blasphemous assumption of the name of deity.* They entitled themselves "sons of the gods"—a satanic half-truth, since the Scriptures designate royal judges "gods" and "sons of the Most High" (Ps 82:6; Exod 21:6), for they are image-reflectors of God's judicial glory. Angels are

---

1. Heb. *nōaḥ*, "Noah"; *n-ḥ-m*, "comfort."
2. On this and the following paragraph, see "Divine Kingship and Genesis 6:1–4"; *Kingdom Prologue*, 184–89.

also sometimes called "sons of God" or "gods," but according to God's verdict (v. 3) the offenders here were men of mortal flesh. Their offspring (v. 4), the princes of the royal court, were powerful military-political figures, Nephilim and Gibborim (the latter being the term used for King Nimrod in 10:8). The interpretation of the "sons of God" as Sethites who transgressed by marrying Cainite women is unsatisfactory, for the daughters of men (vv. 1, 2) are women in general and such religiously mixed marriages would not explain the peculiar nature of the offspring (v. 4).

A hundred and twenty years (v. 3). God's lawsuit against the world conducted through his Spirit-inspired prophets (cf. 1 Pet 3:19, 20) was reaching its climax. In only 120 years, God would blot out man and his world (cf. v. 7). This division (5:1–6:8) thus reviews the history of the world that then was (2 Pet 3:5, 6) from creation (5:1, 2) to its final judgment, a prophetic paradigm of overall eschatology. God's verdict (6:3) arose from his judgment that the increase of mankind (v. 1) was matched by an increase in human depravity, deep and totally pervasive (v. 5; cf. vv. 11, 12).

The LORD was grieved (v. 5; cf. v. 7), or repented. Obviously, the Omniscient was not caught by surprise; rather, his change of mind indicates a sovereign purpose to reverse what he had done, to unmake what he had made (v. 7; cf. vv. 13, 17).

Noah found favor (v. 8). God's de-creating would involve a redemptive re-creating so that his original ultimate kingdom purposes for creation would still be realized.

DIVISION THREE

Redemptive Judgment and Re-creation (6:9–9:29)

6:9 ▷ **Account of Noah.** Genesis 6:9–9:29, the third section of the book's first triad, presents the redemptive resolution of the conflict of the two lines of mankind previously traced. It tells about the end of the old world in the flood (6:9–8:22) and the inauguration of the present world order, including a prophetic overview of its history (8:20–9:29). Jesus points to this Noahic age, with its climactic episode of de-creation and re-creation, as a typological pattern of the day of the Lord (Matt 24:37; Luke 17:26; cf. 2 Pet 3:5–7).

Covenant of Salvation with Noah (6:9–8:22)

6:9–12 ▷ The narrative of re-creation through deluge reflects in many respects the literary form of the original creation account. It has seven sections, distinguished by differing themes, that overlap chronologically. The opening triad deals with de-creation and the entrance of the ark-kingdom into the judgment; the center section, with the judgment crisis; and the closing triad, with the re-emergence of the ark-kingdom in re-creation. More specifically, the concentric outline is:

  A. Construction (6:13–22)
    B. Embarkation (7:1–5)
      C. Increasing Waters (7:6–12)
        D. Prevailing of Waters (7:13–24)
      C′. Decreasing Waters (8:1–14)
    B′. Disembarkation (8:15–19)
  A′. Consecration (8:20–22)

Genesis 6:9–12 is equivalent to the introduction in the creation prologue in 1:2. Each introduction presents a contrast between a problematic situation and a promising presence. Corresponding to the empty earth of chaotic deep and darkness is an earth full of violent men and corruption (vv. 11, 12). Corresponding to the Spirit who would bring forth the cosmic kingdom is the figure of Spirit-prophet Noah (v. 9; cf. note on 5:22, 24), a hint of the emergence of the ark-kingdom from the corrupt world and chaotic waters.

A righteous man (v. 9). Noah had been a faithful prophet and continued his obedience in this new mission (cf. 6:22; 7:5). Because of his righteous acts there would be salvation for his family from the coming judgment (see 7:1; cf. Heb 11:7). Consistent with this is the statement that "Noah found favor in the eyes of the LORD" (v. 8), for that does not refer to mercy received in spite of ill desert, but to approbation for faithful service (cf. Gen 39:4). In the typological deluge-judgment, Noah was a type of Christ, whose righteousness secures eternal salvation for his people.

6:13–22 ▷ Reflecting the fiat-fulfillment format of the day-sections of Gen 1 is the command-fulfillment pattern of this and other sections of the deluge record; thus, command is found in vv. 13–21 and its fulfillment is found in v. 22. Noah's commissioning has two balancing parts (vv. 12–16 and 17–21), each with warning of judgment (vv. 13 and 17) followed by directives concerning, respectively, the ark's construction (vv. 14–16) and its occupants and provisioning (vv. 18–21).

Destroy the earth (v. 13) ... **all life** (v. 17). A worldwide flood seems to be indicated by the comprehensive terms used here for its purpose (cf. 7:4) and afterward for its actual effects (7:19–23; cf. 8:21; 9:11, 15). But dogmatism must be restrained, for sometimes Scripture uses universal-sounding terms for more limited situations (cf. Dan 2:38; 4:22; 5:19), and a local perspective is evident at the critical descriptive point in the flood narrative (see note on 7:17–20). Still, the Gen 10 account of the repopulating of the world shows a vast area had been devastated, and Peter's cosmic language suggests at least the severing of the central trunk of human history (2 Pet 3:5–7).

Make an ark (v. 14). As the vehicular means of preservation through the flood, the ark was a seaworthy structure. Yet it had the form of a house, and in this respect it was a symbolic reproduction of the cosmos viewed as God's temple or royal house.[1] Scripture figuratively depicts the cosmos as a house of three stories, with a window in the heavenly story through which the waters above rain down (cf. 7:11; 8:2) and a door barring the waters below (Job 38:8–11; cf. Gen 7:11; 8:2). Precisely the same architectural features were prescribed by the Creator-Masterbuilder of the heavenly city-house (cf. Prov 8:30; Heb 11:10) for the ark (6:14–16; 8:6). The Lord revealed to Noah the pattern of this house of God, as he later disclosed to Moses and Solomon the designs of the tabernacle and temple. Completing the cosmic creation in miniature, representatives of the vegetable and animal worlds as well as of the human family were brought into the ark, an arrangement with the practical purpose of preserving these creaturely kinds and feeding the ark occupants (6:19–21).

---

1. *Kingdom Prologue*, 225–27; *Glory in Our Midst*, 149–51.

I will establish my covenant (v. 18a). In the parallelism of the two-part commissioning, this covenant corresponds to the provision of the ark of salvation in v. 14. Hence it is at once expounded by the stipulation for entering the ark (v. 18b). It is God's arrangement for deliverance from the deluge doom just threatened (v. 17; cf. v. 13). By this covenant, God commits himself to save the community that was calling on his name and to bestow on them his holy kingdom, in the ark. Covenant is seen here to be a transaction with divinely sanctioned commitment, instrumental in the administration of God's dominion. In particular, this was a covenant grant to faithful Noah (see note on 6:4), like those given by ancient sovereigns to loyal vassals for meritorious service. Membership in this ark covenant, as in all redemptive administrations, was in terms of the family authority structure; hence, Noah's wife and his sons and their wives were included (6:18b; 7:1, 7, 13). God established (v. 18), i.e., fulfilled, this salvation covenant in the course of the flood (see note on 8:1). Not to be confused with this covenant is the common grace covenant with all mankind formalized after the flood-salvation episode (see notes on Gen 9).

7:1–5 ▷ Again the format is command (vv. 1–4) and execution (v. 5). The gathering of the elect, harvesting them into the heavenly garner, is a prominent feature of the final day of the Lord (Matt 3:12; 24:31; 2 Thess 2:1; Rev 14:14–16). The prototype of this in the flood, the gathering into the ark-kingdom, is the theme of this second section (vv. 1–3) and is repeated at the beginning of the next two sections (7:7–9 and 7:13–16). In the coming of the animals to Noah, God's hand can be discerned. He is the ultimate Gatherer.

Clean . . . unclean (v. 2). This distinction identifies the ark order as a holy theocracy, like later theocratic Israel, where the distinction reappears. The extra clean animals provided for food in the ark and sacrifice afterward (cf. 8:20). Oblivious to the momentous separation taking place between the saved and the damned, earthlings pursued their common affairs to the last day (Matt 24:37–39).

7:6–12 ▷ After the theme of the seven-days gathering is repeated, correlated now with Noah's age (vv. 6–9), the forty days of increasing waters of the flood proper are described (vv. 10–12).

Springs of the great deep . . . floodgates of the heavens (v. 11). The unleashing and merging of these two water sources was a veritable reversal of the bounding of the deep by the separation of the waters above and below on creation day two (cf. 1:6, 7).

7:13–24 ▷ Leading into the theme of the prevailing of the waters is a restatement of both the previous themes, the gathering into the ark (vv. 13–16) and the forty-days increasing of the waters (vv. 17ff.). The heaping up of themes in successive sections from one to two to three mirrors the phenomenon of the mounting flood. As the waters rose, they prevailed over the ark by setting it afloat (v. 17) and carrying it where they would (v. 18). Cresting, they covered the mountains (vv. 19, 20), and by prevailing over that final refuge they prevailed over all breathing land creatures outside the ark, particularly man (vv. 21–23). The twenty feet (v. 20) corresponds to the draft of the ark and refers to the depth necessary for the ark to be set afloat (v. 17) or to clear the mountains over which it moved (v. 19). In either case, the perspective being local, what v. 20 affirms cannot without more ado be extrapolated into a global observation.

Only . . . in the ark (v. 23). Escape was found in no other place under heaven (cf. Acts 4:12) except the refuge the Lord designed and personally secured (v. 16). By fastening the door, he barred the death waters and shut out the unrepentant, ending the day of grace (cf. Matt 25:10–13). Isaiah equated the enclosure in the ark with the experience of death for God's people (Isa 16:20; cf. Rev 14:13; 20:4–6); both are sanctuaries from the wrath of God abroad in the world. Peter identified the flood as a baptism (1 Pet 3:21), a passage through the waters of death. In Christ, the ark, there is safe passage; the prevailing waters are themselves overcome in resurrection, swallowed up in victory (Isa 25:8; 1 Cor 15:54). By prevailing over the world city and its anti-God rulers, the flood-judgment saved the godly remnant from extermination. Discriminating as it did between godly and ungodly, and being the means of salvation for believers, the flood was a redemptive judgment, not a common curse visitation but an intrusive prototype of final judgment. The conflicting claims of the two seeds to world inheritance were settled in the ordeal waters, which condemned, dispossessed, and executed the serpent's seed but saved, enriched, and vindicated the woman's seed (cf. Heb 11:7; 1 Pet 3:20).

A hundred and fifty days (v. 24). The period of prevailing overlapped the forty days of the flood proper (cf. 7:11, 12, 17; 8:3, 4), while the last 110 days of prevailing were in turn overlapped by the period of decreasing waters (8:1–14), which began at the end of the forty days of increasing (cf. 8:2, 3).

8:1–14 ▷ **God remembered Noah** (v. 1). To fulfill previous covenantal commitments is called "remembering" the covenant, or the recipient of the covenant promise (cf. Exod 2:24; 32:13; Luke 1:72, 73). God's promised salvation (see note on 6:18) was now carried out in the triumphant reemergence of the ark-kingdom from the judgment, as described in the closing triad of the seven-sectioned flood story.

He sent a wind (v. 1). The forty-day process of de-creation had replicated the chaotic deep of Gen 1:2, and the Spirit of that verse is alluded to at the beginning of this re-creation, wind and Spirit being the same in Hebrew.² Re-creation at once repeated the accomplishment of day two of creation by reconfining the upper and lower waters (v. 2). From this point on, the waters decreased and eventually ceased to prevail (the negative counterpart to the process of re-creation).

The ark came to rest (v. 4). Previous reappearance of the mountain whose slopes were the ark's landfall terminated the waters' prevailing over the mountains. Their prevailing over the ark, and indeed the entire 150 days of prevailing (cf. 7:24), ended with this settling of the ark. (Their prevailing over the ungodly in death was, of course, not reversed.) The verb "rested" puns on Noah's name.³ This outcome registered decisively God's favorable verdict in the ordeal of judgment. Noah had prevailed over the waters and the satanic world power, and had become the savior of his people.

Mountains of Ararat (v. 4), ancient Urartu, later Armenia, was an area strategically central with a view to waves of emigration repopulating the Near Eastern world of the Bible.

Continued to recede (v. 5). The waters' recession continued beyond the end of their prevailing, with the land re-emerging ever lower on the surrounding slopes (vv. 5ff.), until the dove brought evidence of even vegetation (v. 11). This was the equivalent of day three of creation (1:9–12). Removal of the covering from the ark (v. 13) let in the daylight and provided sight of the heavens, evocative of days one (1:3–5) and four (1:14–18), while one may see in the flights of the raven and dove (vv. 6–12) a return of the birds of day five (1:22) to their sky-realm of day two.

8:15–19 ▷ Here again the pattern is command (vv. 15–17) and obedience (vv. 18, 19).

---

2. Heb. *rûaḥ*.
3. Heb. *nōaḥ*, "Noah"; *n-w-ḥ*, "rest."

Come out of the ark (v. 15) is a counterpart to "Go into the ark" in the parallel second section (7:1). The Lord's command was a summons to the dead to come forth from the grave (John 11:43; 5:28, 29), for the ark was a veritable burial chamber in the passage through the death waters (see comment on Isa 26:20 in note on 7:22), an intermediate state. The uncovering of the ark and coming forth (v. 18) was symbolic of the resurrection of the saints. This ark company, the preserved remnant, was now the victorious remnant; prototypes of the overcomers who inherit the eternal temple-city (Rev 21:7); the community of glorified mankind; the new humanity of gods in the image of God, their dominion (under God) over the cosmos perfected.

All the animals (v. 19). Reappearance of animals and man on the dry ground, henceforth to multiply in the earth (v. 17), paralleled the sixth creation day (1:24–27).

Common Grace Covenant
(8:20–9:17)

8:20-22 ▷ **Built an altar** (v. 20). Construction of the ark, symbol of God's cosmic house, in the first section of the flood account (6:13–22) is paralleled in this seventh section by the construction of an altar, symbol of the mountain of God, site of his temple. As a priest-king, type of the second Adam, the true man, triumphant Noah consecrated his kingdom in token sacrifices to the King of kings, who had subjected the world to him (cf. 1 Cor 15:24–28). The Lord took pleasure in his finished re-creation thus consecrated to him. Here is a clear equivalent of the seventh day of the original creation (1:31; 2:1, 2). The portrayal of re-creation in the episode symbolic of final judgment was complete, a prophecy of the new heaven and earth beyond the fiery end of the present heavens and earth (2 Pet 3:7, 13).

Division Three: Redemptive Judgment and Re-creation (6:9–9:29)   41

Genesis 8:20–22 does double duty; it is the closing section of the deluge narrative and the opening A-section of an A.B.A´-structured record of the postdiluvian covenant of common grace (8:20–9:17). What transpired in the flood was only a sign of the consummation and world to come. The interim world of common grace and common curse went on, and the Lord proceeded at once to reinstitute the order of man's common cultural task with its institutions of family and state. The stabilizing of nature is the subject of the opening (8:20–22) and concluding (9:8–17) A-sections. The central B-section (9:1–7) presents regulations for the cultural sphere.

As long as the earth endures (v. 22). This covenant does not bestow the eternal kingdom but is a temporal interim arrangement. God's providential ordering of nature will not permit another catastrophe on the scale of the deluge until the final judgment itself.

9:1–7 ▷ This central section itself has a concentric pattern. It begins (v. 1) and closes (v. 7) with the family function of procreation; the middle (vv. 2–6) deals with man's dominion, general (vv. 2–4) and special, i.e., the state (vv. 5, 6). The family is made the framework. It is the primary institution in the common cultural program. The state is supplementary and should be supportive of the family.

The fear of you (v. 2). The noun is used for reverence to God (Isa 8:12, 13; Mal 1:6). Man's God-like dignity of lordship over the animal world is perpetuated under common grace. This includes the use of animal flesh for food. In the theocratic kingdom in the ark, as in theocratic Israel, only clean meats could be eaten. But with this reestablishment of the common grace order, the theocratic restriction is removed: "I now give you all" kinds of meat again (v. 3; cf. Acts 10:11–15).

Its lifeblood (v. 4). In the context of altar symbolism, the blood of sacrificed animals is a ransom-equivalent for human life forfeit to God through sin. Within this sphere of the earthly altar, even in the non-theocratic world of the patriarchs, this limitation prohibiting the ingestion of blood was placed on common provisions.

By man shall his blood be shed (v. 6). The state is reinstituted in terms reflective of the original charter of the city (cf. 4:15), the focus again on its judicial function as God's servant, bearing the sword as an agent to punish the wrongdoer (cf. Rom 13:1–4; 1 Pet 2:13, 14).

Image of God (v. 6). Man's investment with such solemn judicial authority was an expression of his God-likeness, as preserved through common grace.

9:8–17 ▷ Covenant between me and the earth (v. 13). God's promise to preserve the fundamental ecological cycles (8:21, 22; 9:11, 15), together with man's cultural order thus made possible (9:1–7), was formalized as a covenant, sealed with a sign (9:12–17). It is an administration of God's general rule over his world, but not a redemptive arrangement bestowing his holy kingdom realm on an elect people. It is, rather, made with all mankind, unbelievers as well as the faithful, with all subhuman creatures, and with the earth itself. Though "everlasting" (v. 16) in the sense of continuing through "all generations" (v. 12), it is limited to the history of this world, being terminated by the final judgment and the inauguration of the world to come (see note on 8:22). The **rainbow in the clouds** (v. 13) pictures God's battle-bow, used in the flood-storm to shoot his shafts of wrath on the earth, now suspended in a condition of peace, a sign that the divine warrior is governing rebellious mankind with forbearance for a season.

I will remember (v. 15; cf. note on 8:1). Commitment in this covenant was only on God's part. Obedience to its cultural regulations (9:1–7) was not a condition for the continuance of this common grace order to its appointed terminus.

Kingdom Oracle
(9:18–29)

9:18, 19 ▷ **Sons of Noah** (v. 18). This anticipates the more immediate introduction to Gen 10:1–11:9 in 10:1, the oracle of Noah being inserted between (9:20–27).

9:20–27 ▷ **Ham saw . . . and told** (v. 22). Ham's behavior betrayed likeness to Satan, who contrived to expose shameful nakedness (3:5, 7).

Covered . . . nakedness (v. 23). Shem and Japheth showed themselves to be the godly seed of the woman by emulating God, who covered nakedness (3:21). Noah's oracle (vv. 25–27), like the Lord's declaration in 3:14, 15, stands at the threshold of a world-age and broadly outlines redemptive history down to the messianic age. Both utterances are primarily curses against satanic wickedness (cf. 9:24), yet they include prophecies of the blessings of redemptive covenant through the conquest of Satan's seed by the woman's seed.

Cursed be Canaan (v. 25; cf. 9:18). In each case, a notable historical curse or blessing is envisaged that will befall a distant generation of some branch of the person's descendants. In Ham's case, the curse specifies the particular branch. There is a pun on the idea of subjugate in Canaan's name.[4] The reference is to God's judgment on the Canaanites executed by Israel's holy war of conquest (cf. Deut 9:3; Judg 4:23; Neh 9:24). For Canaan to be servant to his brothers (vv. 25–27) signifies rejection from the covenant of salvation (cf. Gen 25:23; Rom 9:12, 13).

Blessed be the Lord, the God of Shem (v. 26): a blessing in doxology form. It puns on Shem, which means "name." His

---

4. Heb. *kěnaʿan*, "Canaan"; *k-n-ʿ*, "subjugate." The verb *k-n-ʿ* is not actually present in this context, however, the first biblical occurrence of it being found in Lev 26:41.

blessing is that the Lord connects his name with Shem's name, identifying himself as "God of Shem." This took place especially in the covenant the Lord made with Shem's descendant Abraham, to whom Melchizedek applied this doxological benediction (cf. 14:19, 20). Abraham's descendants dispossessed the Canaanites but brought blessing to all the nations of the earth in the person and work of Abraham's messianic seed, the champion-savior seed of the woman.

May Japheth live in the tents of Shem (v. 27). Shem and Japheth had performed their godly service for Noah in his tent (cf. vv. 21–23), and the oracle pictures them together in the same tents. This blessing begins, "May God open [a verb that puns on the sound of Japheth] for Japheth,"[5] the object "tents" being provided in the next clause. Though the gentiles were in old covenant days strangers to the covenants of promise given to Semite Abraham, in the messianic age multitudes out of all nations join the remnant of Israel in the tents of the new covenant. In particular, God opened the door for the Japhetic gentiles in the mission of the apostle Paul (cf. Acts 14:27; 1 Cor 16:8).

9:28, 29 ▷ The third division of Genesis concludes, as it began (6:9, 10), with genealogical data, which complete the formula in Gen 5:32.

---

5. Heb. *p-t-h*, "open"; *yepet*, "Japheth." The pun is particularly striking in that the consonants of the form "may he open" (*ypt*, vocalized *yapt*) are identical to the consonants of the name Japheth (*ypt*, vocalized *yepet*).

DIVISION FOUR

CITY OF MAN IN THE NEW WORLD
(10:1–11:9)

DIASPORA OF MANKIND
(10:1–32)

10:1 ▷ Shem, Ham and Japheth. The second triad of the ten divisions of Genesis (comprising divisions four through six, 10:1–25:11), like the first (comprising divisions one through three, 2:4–9:29), begins with the theme of the city of man, introduced here, at the beginning of the fourth division (10:1–11:9), by this superscription. Though evidencing God's common grace, the process of repopulating the earth is viewed here as a scattering, separating effect of the common curse. This exile-diaspora aspect is highlighted by the representative Babel episode appended (11:1–9). Most of the "sons" listed are collective groups. Some could trace roots to more than one Noahic line because of early intermixtures. The descendants number seventy, a conventional total (cf. 46:27; Exod 1:5), which is indicative of a selective genealogy, as in Gen 5 and 11:10ff. Developments are sketched in each Noahic line so as to suggest how the destinies predicted in the preceding oracle (9:25–27) were taking shape.

10:2-5 ▷ Sons of Japheth (v. 2). Fulfillment of Noah's blessing on Japheth (9:27) would be particularly through Paul's gentile mission to the northwest of the Holy Land. Japheth's line is identified with nations in that area.

Maritime peoples (v. 5), or coastland nations, is the term Isaiah uses for gentiles awaiting the light of messianic salvation (11:11; 24:15; 42:4; 49:1; 51:5; cf. Acts 13:47). Japhetic Magog (v. 2), however, was the location of the "Olympus" site of antichrist Gog (cf. Ezek 38 and 39; Rev 20:8). Noah's oracle did not mean that all Japhetic and Semitic peoples were elect and all Hamites reprobate.

Territories ... clans ... nations ... language (v. 5; cf. vv. 20, 31). Subgroupings within the three Noahic branches were differentiated in these respects.

10:6-20 ▷ Sons of Ham (v. 6). Ham's migration from Ararat was southward, especially southwest. His primary descendants are listed from Cush, south of Egypt, northwards (v. 6).

Sons of Cush (v. 7) extended into Arabia (v. 7) and Mesopotamia (vv. 8-12). The lines of Mizraim and Cush produced major antagonists of Israel. Babylon, in Shinar (cf. 11:1-9), rival world center to Jerusalem (cf. Dan 1:2; Zech 5:11), is identified with the beginning of Cushite Nimrod's kingdom (v. 10).

Nimrod ... mighty warrior (v. 8). This designation links him to the evil tyrants of 6:4, suggesting resurgence of the anti-God spirit of the old world.

Assyria (v. 11), cruel nation that took Israel captive, is also traced to Nimrod (cf. Mic 5:6 [Heb. 5]).

Mizraim (v. 13) is Egypt, infamous house of bondage. From this line derived the Philistines (v. 14), another bitter foe of Israel.

Canaan (v. 15), explicitly targeted in Noah's curse, is identified with groups found in lists of peoples occupying the promised land and dislodged by Israel (vv. 15–18; cf. Gen 15:19–21; Exod 23:23; Deut 7:1; Josh 3:10). The sketch of Canaan's boundaries (v. 19) anticipates later delineations of the land promised in the Abrahamic Covenant. Mention of the Jebusites (v. 16) is an intimation of the future city of God, for Jebus was an earlier name of Jerusalem (Judg 19:10; 1 Chr 11:4), the redemptive restoration of Eden's mountain of God, God's answer to Nimrod's Babylon. Also in the territory of cursed Canaan were the doomed cities of the plain (v. 19).

10:21–31 ▸ **Sons . . . to Shem** (v. 21). A genealogy of Shem is included here in the general survey of nations, but another follows, in 11:10–26, devoted to the elect line. They have in common Shem's descendants from Arphaxad to Eber (10:24; 11:10–15), father of Peleg and Joktan (v. 25). Here (vv. 26–30) the Joktan branch, which bypasses Abraham, is followed, but 11:16–26 traces the elect branch of Peleg.

Ancestor of all the sons of Eber (v. 21). This points to Abraham and the fulfillment of Noah's blessing on Shem through him, for "Hebrew," familiar ethnic designation of Abraham (14:13), is the gentilic of Eber.

Peleg . . . divided (v. 25), another name-pun,[1] refers to the Joktan-Peleg division of the Eberites into rejected and elect lines. The distribution of the sons of Shem from Ararat was to be south, especially the southeast. The Joktan groups (vv. 26–30) were located in south Arabia.

ESCALATION OF EVIL IN BABEL (11:1–9)

11:1–9 ▸ The Babel enterprise reveals the inner religious spirit of the expansion of mankind that Gen 10 described in

---

1. Heb. *peleg*, "Peleg"; *p-l-g*, "divide."

its outward aspects. This episode is connected with Nimrod by the common location, **Shinar** (11:2; cf. 10:10), and common theme, the origin of Babylon (cf. 10:10). This indicates that the Babel episode transpired well along in the millennia between Noah and Abraham. It is, then, not an account of the first differentiation of speech after the flood (cf. 10:5, 20, 31), but of a special local instance of such, effected supernaturally.

11:1–4 ▷ **Whole world** (v. 1), or land; either meaning is possible. If, as in 10:32, it is "earth," v. 1 would describe the situation not long after the flood; but vv. 2ff., a much later situation. However, it may have the restricted meaning in v. 1 found in v. 2 (land of Shinar). This is also suggested by the usage in vv. 8, 9.

Eastward (v. 2). The context of the founding of both Cain's city and Babel is dispersed mankind wandering in the east (cf. 4:16).

Tower . . . to the heavens (v. 4). Exiled from Eden and its holy cosmic mountain, they would construct from the cursed ground upward their own staircase-mountain to the gods. Such were the ziggurats.

Not be scattered (v. 4). Their rallying cry recalls Cain's complaint (4:14) in its impatience with the curse of lost focus and cohesion in man's cultural expansion toward global fullness.

Let us build (v. 4). The Lord was going to restore the paradise order with its mountain of God (cf. Sinai and Zion, type and antitype) as a gift of redemptive grace, but they attempted to gain immortality by their own work.

A name for ourselves (v. 4). This resumes the ancient quest for superhuman name. The ideological kinship of Babel and the Gen 6:1–4 situation is suggested by Nimrod's role at Babel.

11:5–9 ▷ Let us go down (11:7): a judicial advent from the heights to which Babel's tower vainly aspired, like God's descent to judge Sodom and Gomorrah (cf. 18:21). Angels, customary agents of judgment on a day of the Lord, attend him (cf. 18:1; 19:1, and see notes on 1:26; 3:8).

Confuse their language ... scattered them (11:7, 8). Geographical separation leads naturally to linguistic differentiation. Here the order is reversed as the Lord registers his displeasure with a particularly flagrant eruption of titanic human unbelief.

Called Babel (v. 9). The outcome was just the reverse of their objectives. The common curse of dispersion was intensified, not nullified, and they obtained a name of shame, not a great name. "Babel" puns on the word "confused."[2] By disrupting the precipitous advance of Satan's antichrist program and forestalling final judgment, the Lord was remembering his covenant of common grace (Gen 9) and so providing for an interim history of sufficient length to accomplish his covenant of redemptive grace.

---

2. Heb. *bābel*, "Babel"; *b-l-l*, "confuse."

DIVISION FIVE

Community of Faith in the New World (11:10–26)

Covenant Line of Shem (11:10–26)

11:10–26 ▷ The period from the flood to the Abrahamic age surveyed in the fourth division (10:1–11:9) is covered again in this fifth division, the theme now being the chosen covenantal line.

Account of Shem (11:10). This second genealogy of Shem parts company with the first one (cf. 10:21–31) at the point of bifurcation celebrated by the name of Peleg (see note on 10:25). Its form is in the style of the Gen 5 genealogy of the covenant line of Seth, with age notations for each patriarch before and after his fathering, but without the total life span or notice of death. Luke 3:36 (with LXX) inserts the name Cainan between Arphaxad and Shelah, making this, like Seth's genealogy, a list with ten members, the last having three sons. Here, once more, these conventional totals indicate a selective, not complete, genealogy. If complete, only some three centuries would intervene between the flood and Abraham, a result quite impossible to accept in light of both inner-biblical problems (like many patriarchs listed in 11:10ff. being alive in Abraham's day or even outliving him) and other evidence (like texts from the supposed time of the flood relating the flood as an event of the distant past, or archaeological disclosure of successive occupation of urban sites for thousands of years before Abraham, uninterrupted by the flood). In the period covered by the genealogy, the life spans of the patriarchs reduce from upward of a millennium to about two hundred years (also problematic for a three-hundred-year period). Primarily, this genealogy attests to God's sovereign faithfulness in preserving the community of faith within the city of man with its Nimrods through all these ages. Though not necessarily confined to Shem's messianic line (cf. notes on 5:2–32), the covenant did continue there, proceeding unfailingly to the fulfillment of Noah's blessing-promise to Shem in the covenant with Abraham.

DIVISION SIX

❧※❧

COVENANT WITH ABRAHAM (11:27–25:11)

INTRODUCTION: GENEALOGICAL SOURCES (11:27–32)

11:27 ▷ **Account of Terah.** By using Terah's name rather than Abraham's in the heading to the sixth division (11:27–25:11), the maternal as well as the paternal roots of the twelve tribes of Israel were covered—for Sarah, Rebekah, Leah, and Rachel were, like Abraham, all descendants of Terah. The first three divisions of Genesis closed with a covenant that bestowed God's kingdom on Noah in the ark; the second triad culminates in a covenant that presents the kingdom to Abraham in God's promises. Repeated declarations of these promises and God's oaths of covenant ratification and confirmation dominate this division. In between are accounts of the trying of Abraham's faith by circumstances adverse to occupation of the promised inheritance (esp. 12:6–14:24) and to the obtaining of the necessary heir (esp. 18:1–21:34). Divine deliverances from kings in situations involving land and property (esp. Gen 14) and the eventual miraculous provision of Isaac as heir (27:1, 2) evidenced the sovereign power and faithfulness that assured God's ultimate bestowal of the covenanted kingdom. On the literary structure, see the Introduction.

11:27–32 ▷ The opening section of division six deals with genealogical sources; the closing section (22:50–25:11), with genealogical succession.

Ur of the Chaldeans (v. 28). According to Stephen (Acts 7:2, 4), this was in Upper Mesopotamia. A Khaldu people is referred to in the Ararat region. Haran would lie on a natural route from Urfa in that area to Canaan. Abraham did not, then, come from the Shinar region, location of the Ur usually identified as his native land. Nehemiah 9:6 uses the language of Israel's deliverance from Egypt (namely, election and exodus) for God's bringing Abraham from Ur to Canaan.

Abram, Nahor and Haran (v. 27). If Haran was the oldest son, the 135 years between Terah's fathering him at the age of seventy (cf. 11:26) and dying at 205 (11:32) would allow reasonably for the facts that he marries and has a daughter who marries and that he dies before Terah (11:27–29). According to Stephen (Acts 7:4), Abraham left the city of Haran after Terah's death. Since Abraham was then seventy-five (Gen 12:4), his birth would be sixty years after Haran's, when Terah was 130.

Sarai was barren (v. 30). A natural obstacle existed in the genealogical sources of the promised seed; fulfillment of the promise would demand the Lord's supernatural intervention. The stay in Haran (v. 31) was a delay in progress with respect to the promise of the land of Canaan contained in the divine call issued to Abraham in Ur (cf. note to 12:1–5).

Promised Inheritance (12:1–15:20)

Covenant Promise and Demand (12:1–5)

12:1–5 ▷ Abraham's summons to his remarkable role in covenant history came before the family left Ur (Acts 7:2ff.; cf. Gen 15:7; Neh 9:7).

Leave your father's household (v. 1). Like the "Follow me" call of Jesus to his disciples, God's summons to Abraham required leaving family and the service of all idols (cf. Mark 10:28f.; John 12:25; 1 Thess 1:9). Terah's household had worshipped idols (Josh 24:2). Through an arrangement of divine grace, not human works, the Abrahamic Covenant entailed human obligations. The salvation it provided is unto holy life and loving service (cf. Gen 18:19).

I will bless you; I will make your name great (v. 2). This prophetic revelation of covenant sanctions applied to Abraham the name-blessing of Noah on Shem (cf. 9:26), with the attendant privilege of mediating blessing to the Japhetic world (cf. 9:27).

All peoples on earth would be blessed through Abraham (v. 3). More specifically, the blessing of the gentiles would be through Abraham's "seed" (cf. 22:13; 26:4; 28:14), one with the champion seed of the woman (3:15), Christ, the second Adam (cf. Gal 3:16).

I will make you into a great nation (v. 2). This promise would have a provisional fulfillment in the Israelite kingdom in Canaan, as the Lord cursed those who cursed Israel, so executing Noah's curse on Canaan (see note on 9:25). Beyond that temporal type, Abraham perceived the permanent fulfillment in the heavenly kingdom that was the goal envisaged from the beginning under the Covenant of Creation (cf. Heb 11:10, 16). In these divine promissory commitments, the heart of covenant was present even though formal ratification would await until later.

Abram left . . . as the Lord had told him (v. 4). This recalls the command-obedience pattern of the flood narrative (see note on 6:13–22) and prepares for the theme of the covenant of grant to Abraham, a supplementary element within this basic covenant of grace arrangement (see notes on 22:1, 18; 26:5).

Difficulties and Deliverance (12:6–13:17)

Circumstances contrary to the land promise confronted Abraham: the presence of the Canaanites, the famine necessitating departure to Egypt, the inability of the land to support him and Lot together. A threat to his wife and thus his promised heir also arose. Yet there was deliverance from this threat, prosperous return to Canaan, and renewal of the divine promises. Similar problems (again involving Sarai and Lot), deliverance, and promises are found in the structurally parallel section 18:1–19:38 (see the Introduction).

12:6–9 ▷ **I will give this land** (v. 7). Territory and people were involved in the "great nation" promise (12:2). The prototypal kingdom territory was gradually defined more precisely (cf. 13:14–17; 15:18–21). An obstacle to its acquisition was the Canaanites already there (v. 6). The Lord would have to remove them (cf. 9:25).

The Lord appeared to Abram (v. 7; cf. 17:1; 18:1; 26:2, 24; 35:9; 48:3). Special confirmation of God's presence steeled Abraham's faith. Theophany during the patriarchal age took the form of the Angel of the Lord (cf. note on 16:7).

He built an altar ... and called on the name of the Lord (vv. 7, 8). In contrast to the Babelites, who built a pseudo-mountain of God to exalt the name of man (11:4), Abraham built a symbolic mountain of God, pointing to the true one that God would provide, and exalted the name of the Lord (cf. note on 4:26). The altars erected at Shechem and Bethel on this first passage through Canaan claimed it as the Lord's holy domain and expressed faith in God's promise to grant it to his elect.

Abram set out and continued (v. 9). It was not time to dispossess the Canaanites. This was an age of common grace, and the patriarchs must be patient pilgrims in this world.

12:10–20 ▷ Went down to Egypt (v. 10). Even resident alien status in the promised land was denied to Abraham. Famine occasioned this Egyptian sojourn, as it would Israel's. Egypt was well watered, like Eden (cf. 13:10).

They will kill me (v. 12). The political conditions Abraham feared in pharaonic Egypt resembled the Gen 6:1–4 crisis, with its divine kingship ideology, royal harem, and violence. Abraham's strategy of deception (vv. 11–13) was arguably defendable, but while partially successful and resulting in an increase of his estate (v. 16), it did not prevent the intolerable situation of Sarah's induction into Pharaoh's harem (v. 15).

The Lord inflicted serious diseases (v. 17). Divine intervention brought escape from the predicament (cf. Ps 105:14, 15). This pharaoh responded more readily to monitory plagues (vv. 18–20) than the one Moses dealt with. In both cases, however, the Lord obliged the world monarch to free and send away his people, enriched with wealth gained from the Egyptian oppressors (cf. 15:14; Exod 12:36). Recalling this earlier deliverance of Abraham, the Israelites in bondage might confidently anticipate their redemption.

13:1–17 ▷ This chapter opens (vv. 1–4) and closes (vv. 14–18) with land claims. Resumed in vv. 5–13 is the theme of the narrowing down of Terah's family to Abraham as the one patriarchal fount of the chosen community, intertwined with the theme of obstacles to the realization of the covenant promises.

13:1–4 ▷ Very wealthy (v. 2). Abraham's assurance of his special vocation in relation to the future of God's kingdom was sustained by the providential ordering of his ways that resulted in success in his commercial affairs (cf. 12:5, 16).

From Egypt to the Negev . . . to Bethel (vv. 1, 3). In Abraham's return to Canaan, Israel's acquisition of the promised land was foreshadowed. Though his entry was not by conquest, at the Bethel altar Abraham reasserted the Lord's claim on the land (v. 4), and thus his own by virtue of covenant promise.

13:5–13 ▷ **Canaanites and Perizzites were also living in the land** (v. 7; cf. 12:6, 8). God's day of judgment was delayed (cf. 15:16); available space for resident aliens was limited. The very prosperity of Abraham and Lot aggravated the problem: **the land could not support them** (v. 6). Confidence in the Lord was evidenced in the magnanimous proposal of the patriarchal peacemaker (vv. 8, 9; cf. 21:22–34).

Lot . . . set out toward the east (v. 11). The narrative of Lot's departure toward Sodom prepares for the episodes of the cities of the plain in Gen 14 and 18–19. Lot was the only other male Terahite who continued from Haran to Canaan (13:5; cf. 12:28–31). His removal now left Abraham to be the exclusive recipient of the covenant promises (cf. 13:14ff.) and sole paternal source of the covenant family (cf. Isa 51:1, 2), a role in which he was a prototype of the Messiah, the second Adam.

13:14–17 ▷ God renewed his covenant commitment to bless Abraham with the kingdom people and land (cf. 12:2, 3, 7).

Look north and south, east and west (13:14). Moses was similarly invited to a panoramic overview of the entire land (Deut 34:1–4). In each case, the Lord was confirming the land promise to one who would not personally participate in the dispossessing of the Canaanites.

Walk through the length and breadth of the land (v. 17). This was evidently a symbolic legal procedure for staking out a land claim (cf. Josh 18:4; 24:3). It did not secure immediate ownership of Canaan for Abraham, but vividly reinforced God's guarantee to give it to his offspring (v. 15).

Forever (13:15; cf. 17:8; 48:4). This is an intimation of the antitypical level of meaning in the covenant promises; for

earthly Canaan is not eternal, but the consummate inheritance of the saints in the new heavens and earth is forever.
Offspring like the dust (v. 16). The promise of kingdom people is renewed in terms echoed in later repetitions of the promise (28:14; cf. 15:5; 16:10; 32:12) and statements of its fulfillment in Israel (Num 23:10; 2 Chr 1:9; 1 Kgs 4:20) and in the new covenant people, Jews and gentiles of all nations, blessed in Abraham's messianic seed (cf. Rom 4:16–18; Gal 3:29; Rev 7:9).

Success and Dedication (13:18–14:24)

This section is bounded by references to Mamre at Hebron (13:18 and 14:24; cf. 14:13). As Abraham's allegiance to his heavenly Suzerain was declared in oath and demonstrated in deed, the Lord revealed his favor toward his vassal by providential protection in warfare and through Melchizedek's priestly pronouncement. This divine-human covenant is seen developing here in a context full of political and military covenants: the suzerainty covenant of Kedorlaomer with his western vassals, the coalition of the four eastern kings, the confederation of the five kings of the plain, and the alliance of Abraham with the Amorite leaders. Adumbrating the future domination of the covenant nation by the Neo-Babylonian power and its successors, this episode manifested God's power to overcome the beast nations and restore his people.

13:18–14:4 ▷ **At Hebron** (13:18). More permanently settled, Abraham erected another altar-claim to Canaan, indeed to the world (cf. Rom 4:13). Large trees at cultic centers might serve as mountain of God symbols, bonds between heaven and earth.
They rebelled (14:4). The region Lot had chosen was under foreign suzerainty and became the object of a punitive attack

(14:2), presumably for refusing payment of the stipulated annual tribute. Though Kedorlaomer was leader of the eastern coalition (14:4, 5), the king of Shinar in the succession of Nimrod is listed first (14:1) to give a Babelite ideological cast to the enterprise. The campaign would be regarded as a visitation of the covenant curse by the gods invoked as treaty witnesses.

14:5-12 ▷ The four kings marched south along a Transjordan route, invincible against powerful nations that were also involved in an evidently widespread revolt, and continued beyond the Dead Sea into the Negev before circling back (vv. 5–7).

Valley of Siddim (v. 8). By the time Genesis was written, this valley had become a shallow extension of the Dead Sea (cf. v. 3).

Carried off Abram's nephew Lot (v. 12). Many captives were taken (cf. vv. 16, 21) but this one would bring into the fray the vassal of another Suzerain, a Suzerain of suzerains, who also laid claim to Canaan.

14:13-16 ▷ **Abram the Hebrew** (v. 13), i.e., descendant of Eber of Shem's chosen line (see notes on 10:21 and 14:19, 20).

Allied with Abram (v. 13). Though a resident alien, Abraham was a wealthy prince (cf. 23:6) over a community of hundreds of people, with a respectable fighting force at his disposal (v. 14). When the hour for God's judgment on Canaan came, military pacts with Canaanites would be forbidden (cf. Exod 23:32), but this was a time of common grace dealings. The three allies kept their covenant with Abraham, sending their troops with his (cf. v. 24). Abraham used all available resources and resorted to standard strategy, but it was the Lord who delivered his enemies into his hand (cf. v. 20; 12:3). They were denied their prey, and the challenge of their avenging gods (see note on vv. 1, 2) to the Lord's su-

zerainty over his land and people was repelled—a warning to Satan as he plots the final coalition of evil under antichrist Gog of Magog (cf. Rev 16:12–14; 20:7–10).
As far as Hobab (v. 15). Abraham chased them clear out of the promised land.

14:17–24 ▷ Abraham responded to his Overlord's faithfulness with expressions of his covenant loyalty by oath (v. 22) and tithe (v. 20), while rejecting a rival benefactor (vv. 23, 24).
Melchizedek (v. 18) represented the decreasing remnant of true religion in the postdiluvian world outside the Abrahamic line.
Priest of God Most High (v. 18). The divine designations coincide with those of the supreme Canaanite god, but as Abraham recognized, Melchizedek's God was the Lord (v. 22). This double office of priest and king in Salem (apparently Jerusalem, cf. Ps 76:2) is exploited in Scripture as a figure of the priest-king Messiah (cf. Ps 110:4; Heb 6:20ff.). Melchizedek's order was prior and superior to the law and its priesthood (cf. Heb 7:4–10). Hence, the appearance of Jesus as priest of the new covenant after the order of Melchizedek means that the intervening, parenthetical order of the law has been done away with (cf. Heb 7:11–8:13). Fulfillment of the perfect hope of the Abrahamic promises is, therefore, not in terms of the shadowy, now obsolete, Mosaic-Levitical economy, but of the better, endless, new covenant order of reality founded on the Melchizedek-like priesthood of Jesus, Abraham's promised seed (cf. Heb 9:1–10:18).
Blessed be Abram . . . blessed be God (vv. 19, 20). Noah's doxology-benediction on Shem (cf. 9:26) was applied to Abraham, descendant of Shem through Eber, in effect renewing the promises that his seed would possess the land (visiting the curse on Canaan) and bring blessing to all nations (fulfilling the blessing on Japheth).

Abram gave him a tenth (v. 20). The presence in Salem of a true cult and priest of the Lord provided Abraham a means of public witness in rendering the customary tithe as tribute to the Lord. What Kedorlaomer seized as tribute due to him ended up being paid to the true Lord of Canaan, the Creator of heaven and earth. In the oath (v. 22), probably before Melchizedek, Abraham confessed allegiance to the Lord God alone; he insisted he would not allow the evil king of Sodom to assume the suzerain's prerogative of stipulating the disposition of battle spoils (v. 21)—a Satan-like insinuating that he, not the Lord, was Abraham's benefactor (cf. 3:1–6; Luke 22:25).

God's Oath of Ratification (15:1–20)

The covenant initiated by God's sovereign call and expressed in promises is here formally ratified by a divine oath ceremony. Though vv. 1–6 and vv. 7–20 might be construed as one visionary experience narrated in topical rather than simple chronological fashion, there is less difficulty if vv. 1–6 are taken as a separate vision occurring some previous evening. While the promise of a son and heir is the concern in vv. 1–6, the promise of the land, which is more important in the 12:1–15:20 section, becomes central in vv. 7–20.

15:1–6 ▷ **I am your shield** (v. 1), or suzerain-protector (cf. Deut 33:29; 2 Sam 22:3). Agreeably, Abraham called him "Sovereign" (v. 2).

Great reward (v. 1). For his faithful performance of covenant obligations (cf. Gen 14; Neh 9:8), a grant of the typological kingdom was made to Abraham. It is on the basis of Christ's obedience that the eternal kingdom is bestowed as a gift of grace on sinners.

I remain childless (v. 2). The promise of a great name required that Abraham have an heir bearing his name to inherit the kingdom grant. Apparently by virtue of adoption, the household servant Eliezer was heir (vv. 2, 3).

A son . . . will be your heir (v. 4). Legal custom had it that a natural son subsequently born replaced an adopted servant as heir. God insisted the natural obstacles would be overcome and the promise of countless descendants fulfilled (v. 5).

Abram believed the Lord (v. 6), voicing the Amen of faith, and God declared his approbation (v. 6; cf. Neh 9:8).[1] Paul expounds this as justification by faith as opposed to the law's principle of works (Gal 3:6–14). To believe the promise of the birth of an heir from dead sources (cf. Heb 11:11, 12; Rom 4:17–21) was the faith equivalent of believing the gospel of justification and kingdom inheritance through the resurrection of Jesus, our sacrifice, from the dead (Rom 4:22–25). Inheritance received by faith is a gift of grace (Rom 4:16; cf. vv. 4–8).

15:7–20 ▷ At Abraham's request for confirmation of the land promise (vv. 7, 8), the Lord instructed him to arrange for an oath ritual (vv. 9–11). Such cutting up of animals to symbolize the oath-curse explains the Hebrew idiom "to cut (i.e., ratify) a covenant" (cf. Jer 34:18–20).[2] The threatening presence of the vultures above the carcasses (v. 11) spoke of the accursed fate of the unburied. A dreadful darkness of deathlike sleep descended on Abraham (v. 12; cf. v. 17), intensifying the horror of the scene. Before undergoing the ritual, the Lord further explained how and when the land would be possessed (vv. 13–16).

Mistreated four hundred years (v. 13). Beside the 215 years still to be spent by Abraham, Isaac, and Jacob in Canaan (cf. v. 15), four centuries must pass for the Abrahamites

---

1. "Abram's Amen."
2. *Kingdom Prologue*, 2.

in Egypt before they received the kingdom. Israel was not just to evolve into the dominant power in Canaan; the kingdom must come through a supernatural act of divine grace redeeming Israel from slavery (v. 14), a prefiguration of the eternal, messianic salvation. Israel was to gain its inheritance by holy war judgment (cf. 9:25, 26), and that must wait until the Amorite grapes of wrath were ripe (v. 16). On the four centuries to that judgment (vv. 13, 16), compare the 120 years to the flood judgment (cf. 6:3).

Passed between the pieces ... made a covenant (vv. 17, 18; cf. Neh 9:8). God's appearance in the form of an ascending cloud of smoke and a soaring tongue of flame anticipated the double-columned cloud-and-fire theophany of Moses' day, the divine presence that secured the kingdom for Israel. The two columns represented the legs of God. He walked the way of death, summoning that death-curse on himself, if he should fail to keep covenant. As the gospel discloses, the covenant was kept and the promises in their ultimate meaning fulfilled in God's only Son undergoing the death-curse. Christ is the surety of the heavenly inheritance for the true seed of Abraham, Jew and gentile (cf. Heb 6:18). Meanwhile, the Lord's oath assured a realization of the typological kingdom in Canaan, which he more precisely defined in terms of its geographical boundaries (v. 18) and present occupants (vv. 19–21).

Linkage: Genealogical Resources (16:1–16)

This section renews the introduction in 11:27–32 (cf. references to Sarah's barrenness in 11:30 and 16:1) and connects 12:1–15:20 with 17:1–22:19. Provision of the patriarchal heir was critical to completion of the covenant program at both the old and new covenant levels. The patriarchal succession was the link between Abraham and the Israelite people, the promised innumerable descendants at the preliminary kingdom level. And Israel, in turn, was the genealogical line for Messiah, in and through whom the eschatological kingdom would come.

16:1–6 ▷ Impatient with her barrenness after a decade in Canaan (v. 1; cf. v. 16; 12:4), Sarah resorted to the legally recognized expedient of providing a surrogate wife for her husband (v. 2).

Abram agreed to what Sarai said (v. 2). Repetition of the expression used by God in judging Adam's sin (3:17) suggests disapproval of such a human stratagem. A non-supernatural origin of the messianic line would obscure the character of the covenanted salvation as the Lord's sovereign accomplishment and gift. The son thus born to the servant woman (a fruit of Sarah's unbelief) would be expressive of the law principle of works, not of gospel grace (cf. Gal 4:21–27).

You are responsible (v. 5). Sarah could not blame Abraham for the original idea, but did insist that he grant the wife's legal right to requite appropriately the arrogance of a servant woman in this situation (cf. 1 Sam 1:6).

16:7–16 ▷ **Angel of the Lord** (v. 7). As Hagar recognized, the One who appeared was the Lord God (cf. v. 13). For divine designations of this Angel elsewhere, cf., e.g., 18:33; 32:24–30. His is the divine prerogative to forgive sin (Exod 23:21), and his presence sanctifies a site (Exod 3:5; Josh 5:15). Yet he is God's angel-messenger and speaks of the Lord in the third person. What explains this combination is his identity as God the Son manifested in angelic mode.

Go back (v. 9). Hagar's flight to her Egyptian homeland (cf. v. 1) was checked, for the child she carried belonged to Abraham's household. Yet he would not stand in the patriarchal succession (cf. 17:18–21) and is cited by Paul as an example of one who was in the covenant (cf. 17:23–27) but not elect unto life (Rom 9:8, 9; see notes on Gen 25:12–18). Indeed, he became a persecutor of the son of promise and was expelled from the covenant community (cf. 21:8ff.; Gal 4:29, 30).

Descendants . . . too numerous to count (v. 10). In terms of common grace, Ishmael would be prospered, for Abraham's sake (cf. 21:13), becoming a proudly independent nomadic nation (v. 12). His descendants cannot be identified with the countless seed of many nations promised to both Abraham and Sarah (17:16; cf. Gal 4:31). Note the similar tenor of Hagar's thankful response and Mary's praise at her heavenly annunciation (16:11, 13 and Luke 1:48).

Ishmael (v. 15). Abraham followed the Angel's instructions, relayed by Hagar. Perhaps in faith, he applied to his desire for the promised heir the assurance of this name, "God-hears." However, the still unresolved problem of Sarah's barrenness (cf. v. 1) would continue and intensify for another decade and more (v. 16; cf. 17:1, 17).

Promised Heir (17:1–22:19)

Covenant Promise and Demand (17:1–37)

The parallel revelations of the covenant promises, 12:1–5 and 17:1–37 (see the Introduction), each present also the basic demand of discipleship (12:1 and 17:1) and relate an act of obedience (12:4 and 17:28). The focus here is on the heir, and the promise is enforced by meaningful changes in names, by specifying an imminent time of fulfillment, and by sealing the covenant with the sign of circumcision. The words of God, after the introduction (vv. 1, 2), divide into three sections, indicated by "as for me" (v. 4), "as for you" (v. 9), and "as for

Sarai" (v. 15). The account alternates between the subjects of covenant promises (vv. 3–8 and vv. 15–22) and circumcision (vv. 9–14 and vv. 23–27).

17:1, 2 ▷ **I am** (v. 2). The Lord's treaty-like opening self-designation, Shaddai, possibly signifies the One of the Mountain, i.e., the holy mount of the heavenly council, as in Eden (cf. Exod 6:3).[3]
Be blameless (v. 1) was the demand for covenant loyalty.
My covenant (v. 2) is identified in vv. 10 and 13 as circumcision, the full expression being "sign of the covenant" (v. 11). Precisely as circumcision is here denoted as "covenant" and said to be "given" (the literal meaning of the verb at the beginning of v. 2)[4] as a sign of the previously ratified covenant of promise, so the Sabbath is called a covenant, given as a sign of the covenant ratified at Sinai (Exod 31:13, 16, 17).

17:3–8 ▷ On his own part, the Lord confirmed his commitment to fulfill his previous covenant promises. The land promise was mentioned (v. 8) and the central reality of God's protector relationship to his people was affirmed (vv. 7, 8; cf. 15:1), but foremost was the promise of descendants (esp. vv. 4–6; cf. v. 2).
Father of many nations (v. 4). Paul sees this fulfilled in the justification of uncircumcised gentiles by faith apart from the works of the law. They were the spiritual sons of Abraham, who also was justified (cf. Gen 15:6) before he was circumcised (17:24), circumcision being added as a seal of the righteousness of faith he had while still uncircumcised (Rom 4:11, 16, 17; cf. Gal 3:29).

---

3. On the mountain of God in Eden, see *God, Heaven and Har Magedon*, 40–48; *Kingdom Prologue*, 47–49; *Images of the Spirit*, 35–42.
4. Heb. *n-t-n*.

Your name will be Abraham (v. 5; cf. Neh 9:7). A graphic confirmation of the nations promise was given in the change of name from Abram to Abraham, which incorporated the word "many, multitude," yielding the promise-meaning "father of a multitude."[5] Ancient suzerains often gave vassals new royal names (cf. v. 6 and note on v. 15).

Kings will come from you (v. 6). David and his successors fulfilled this promise of royal dynasty; and, in the new covenant, David's greater Son, the King over the multitude of father Abraham's nations, did. Cf. also 17:16; 35:11; 49:10; 2 Sam 7:5–16.

Everlasting covenant . . . possessions (vv. 7, 8). The covenantal kingdom, people, and land were not limited to the passing old covenant order but contemplated Canaan's heavenly antitype and the people out of many nations in Christ, whose kingdom is forever (cf. 2 Sam 7:13).[6]

17:9–14 ▷ On Abraham's part, the covenant required exclusive consecration to the service of his Sovereign (cf. v. 1).

Circumcision (v. 11) was a symbolic oath-pledge of such loyalty. For its dedicatory function, cf. Lev 19:23–25; Jer 4:4. Like the similar knife ritual in the covenant ratification ceremony (15:9ff.), it depicted God's judgment sword inflicting the death-curse. Thus, with obvious allusion to the act of circumcision, the curse of being cut off is threatened against the one who broke this covenant by despising its sign (v. 14). The contextual concern with offspring and the nature of circumcision indicate

---

5. Scholars debate what element of the name Abraham, whether -*rāhām* or simply -*hām*, means "multitude"; some, for example, have pointed to the fact that -*hām* is identical to the beginning of the Hebrew word *hāmôn*, "multitude," but this may not be the best way to explain the meaning of Abraham's name.

6. *Kingdom Prologue*, 332–40; *God, Heaven and Har Magedon*, 97–102.

that the covenant breaker's descendants are included in the excision curse. The one who enters the redemptive covenant by circumcision, or its new covenant equivalent of baptism, is invited to identify by faith with Christ in his circumcision-baptism on the cross (cf. Luke 12:50; Col 2:11) and thus to undergo in him the death judgment we all deserve as covenant-breakers in Adam. This leads to justification and life with Christ in his resurrection-vindication (Rom 6:3–5; Col 2:12; cf. Rom 4:11).

17:15–22 ▷ As for Sarah's role, God declared she would be mother of the heir and the numerous nations, with their kings, promised to Abraham (v. 16), and he renewed her name "Princess" in an alternative form (v. 15; cf. note on v. 5).[7]

He laughed (v. 17). Abraham's laughter, later echoed by Sarah's (18:12), accounts for the promised son's name, Isaac, "Laughter" (v. 19).[8] Whatever ingredients of faith and incredulity informed the parents' laughter, it underscored the natural impossibility (v. 17) of what the Lord promised to do. Isaac's miraculous birth would betoken the supernatural work of grace that would accomplish resurrection from circumcision-death for all the nations promised to father Abraham and mother Sarah.

If only Ishmael might live (v. 18). Though granting this plea by promising Ishmael a twelve-tribe nation (v. 20; cf. 25:16), the Lord emphatically distinguished this destiny from the future program of redemptive covenant appointed to Isaac and his descendants, the twelve tribes of Israel (vv. 19, 21).

This time next year (v. 21). Sarah's laughable prospect would be realized—and without further delay.

---

7. Heb. *śārâ*, "Sarah," which means "princess," has the standard Hebrew feminine ending -*â* and is the normal, expected feminine form of the noun *śar*, "prince." The ending -*ay* in the byform *śāray*, "Sarai," appears to be an archaic feminine ending.

8. Heb. *yiṣḥāq*, "Isaac"; ṣ-ḥ-q, "laugh."

17:23–27 ▷ After the Lord's disappearance into heaven (v. 22), Abraham executed his command (v. 23).

Every male in Abraham's household (v. 23). From the beginning, formation of the covenant community respected the family institution (see notes on 5:1; 6:18; 19:15). As shown by the regulations governing circumcision, membership in the covenant included those under the household authority of the one who confessed faith. Continued into the new covenant, this principle finds expression in the recognition of children under the parental authority of a confessor as "holy" (Rom 11:16; 1 Cor 7:14), in the sense of separated from this profane world and belonging to the covenant community.[9] The basis for their inclusion is not the promise, for the promised seed is the elect seed and non-elect Ishmael and Esau were circumcised. However, the death-curse invoked in the membership oath ritual of circumcision-baptism is experienced in two radically different ways by those who are covenantally holy, depending on whether or not they are holy in Christ (see notes on vv. 9–14).

Difficulties and Deliverance (18:1–19:38)

Cf. notes on the parallel passage, 12:6–13:17. The promises are renewed and there are encouraging evidences of the Lord's presence, but there is keen awareness of the humanly insurmountable obstacles to fulfillment of the promises, particularly the promise of an heir.

18:1–5 ▷ **The Lord appeared** (v. 1). The divine visitation had two purposes: confirmation of the recent specific promise concerning Isaac (18:1–15; cf. 17:21) and judgment on the cities of the plain (18:16–19:29). A connection between the two was that in the destruction of Sodom and its sequel (19:30–38)

---

9. *Kingdom Prologue*, 361–65; *By Oath Consigned*, 90–94.

Division Six: Covenant with Abraham (11:27–25:11)

Lot was removed as a possible heir for Abraham, an option perhaps in Abraham's mind in bringing him from Haran to Canaan (12:4). This left Abraham with no place to look but the Lord of redemptive miracle. (See also the note on 19:30–38.)

Saw three men (v. 2). Abraham addressed one of them as "my Lord" (v. 3, KJV; the title, not the name Yahweh),[10] recognizing the Angel of the Lord, particularly from his very recent appearance (17:1, 22). Hebrews 13:2 does not, then, refer to this episode but another, like 19:1ff. (cf. Judg 13:3ff.). Abraham had responded to earlier divine appearances and promises by building altars and thereon serving the Lord (cf. 12:6–9). Here he served him with the hospitality of his tent. Possibly the meal functioned to seal the covenantal engagement of 17:21.

Sarah laughed (v. 12; cf. 17:7, 9), incredulous at the thought of one procreatively dead (cf. Heb 11:11, 12; Rom 4:19) producing life. The omniscience that perceived the secret laugh (vv. 12, 15; cf. John 1:48–51) suggested the supernatural resources that would accomplish the laughable.

Anything too hard for the LORD? (v. 14). Romans 4:21 indicates that Abraham was persuaded of the right answer (cf. Heb 11:11). His Amen of faith to the same promise of descendants (15:4–6) illustrated the justifying faith of those who believe in him who raised our Lord Jesus from the dead (Rom 4:22–25).[11]

18:16–33 ▷ **Shall I hide from Abraham** (v. 17). Abraham, called a prophet by the Lord (20:7; Ps 105:15), stood in the tradition of Enoch and Noah. Two prophetic features combine here, access to God's council decisions (cf. Jer 23:16–22) and intercession (cf. 20:7; Jer 15:1; 27:18), as the Lord discloses the

---

10. The Masoretic text has *'ădōnāy*, literally, "my lords" (though, if construed as a so-called "plural of majesty," this could be translated "my lord"; cf. the Septuagint, which has the singular *kyrie*).

11. "Abram's Amen," esp. 10–11.

judicial purpose of his mission (vv. 17–21) and Abraham intercedes for Lot's deliverance (vv. 22–32).

To keep the way of the LORD (v. 19). Linked to a restatement of the promises of kingdom and mediation of universal blessing (v. 18; cf. 12:3) was a declaration of the goal of a people renewed in God's image.

Doing what is right and just (v. 19). God's glory of judicial righteousness, the central contextual concern (cf. v. 25), is to be reproduced in his people. Fulfilling this obligation was integral to fulfillment of the promised blessings (v. 19).

The outcry has reached me (v. 20). The Lord's investigative mission was in response to the judicial complaint that had come before his court. The term for outcry puns on the term for right (v. 19).[12] Isaiah, conducting God's lawsuit against Judah, used the same pun in his indictment of them as behaving like Sodom and Gomorrah (Isa 1:10; 5:7; cf. Jer 23:14).[13] The divine judgment on those cities provided a prophetic forewarning of Jerusalem's fall for failure to keep the Lord's way of righteousness (Isa 1:9; Lam 4:6; Rom 9:29; cf. Jude 7).

Will you sweep away the righteous with the wicked? (v. 23; cf. Jer 12:1ff.). Abraham's intercession was in behalf of Lot, and it prevailed (cf. 19:29). He put the sparing of Lot in the form of sparing the city, not anticipating how God would rescue Lot while destroying the city. Simply taking the question as posed, the Lord assured Abraham that in such a special visitation of direct divine judgment (prototypal of final judgment) he does not let the righteous perish.[14] Abraham could

---

12. Heb. *zĕʿāqâ*, "outcry"; *ṣĕdāqâ*, "right."
13. Isaiah 5:7 uses the byform *ṣĕʿāqâ* for "outcry," thus punning on the sounds of *ṣĕdāqâ*, "right," even more closely than *zĕʿāqâ* does in Gen 18:19–20.
14. On the concept of the "intrusion" of final judgment into history, see *The Structure of Biblical Authority*, 154–71.

have reduced the hypothetical remnant to one and received the same commitment from the righteous Judge.

19:1–38 ▷ Narrated here are the exposure of Sodom's evil (vv. 1–14); the deliverance of Lot from Sodom's doom (vv. 15–29); and Lot's divergent line (vv. 30–38).

19:1–14 ▷ **The two angels** (v. 1; cf. 18:2, 22). The Lord himself does not appear after leaving Abraham (18:33); God's words to Lot in 19:21, 22 are probably, therefore, direct quotation. In judgment episodes, angels gather in the elect, saving them from God's wrath (see note on 7:1–5). The two angels were dispatched on the mission that answered Abraham's prayer before he prayed (cf. 18:22).

Lot (v. 1) was identified as a righteous remnant by his Abraham-like hospitality (vv. 2ff.; cf. 18:3ff.; Heb 13:2), one at odds with his lawless neighbors' filthy lives (cf. 2 Pet 2:7).

All the men . . . of Sodom (v. 4). Quickly exposed was the extreme corruption of the whole city, young and old, outside Lot's household (cf. 6:5; 8:21; Rom 1:26–32). The outcry from Sodom (cf. 18:20, 21) was like that before the flood (cf. 6:11) and resulted in another intrusion of special judgment into common grace history.[15] But though like the flood judgment in principle, this one was not so extensive, the Lord being faithful to his postdiluvian covenant with all the earth (8:21, 22).

He wants to play the judge (v. 9). Lot's place in the gateway (v. 1), where the court sat, perhaps indicates a judicial role in local affairs. The Sodomites failed to recognize who it really was that was judging them (cf. 2 Pet 2:6–12). Their resentment at being held judicially accountable further condemned them (cf. 3:8–13).

They struck the men . . . with blindness (v. 11). Divine intervention provided deliverance for Lot and the daughters

---

15. Again, see *The Structure of Biblical Authority*, 154–71.

compromised by his ill-advised suggestion (cf. v. 8), as it did for Abraham and compromised Sarah in Egypt (cf. 12:11–20). By this action and the angels' disclosure of the nature of their mission (v. 13) Lot became aware who it was he entertained.

Thought he was joking (v. 14). Even the prospective sons-in-law found the very idea of divine reckoning laughable (cf. 2 Pet 3:3ff.). Sodom outside Lot's door was without exception reprobate.

19:15–29 ▷ **Take your wife and two daughters** (v. 15). The bounds of the covenant community, which in this prototypal final judgment episode represented the elect (cf. note on 7:1–5),[16] are, as usual, determined by the family structure (cf. 19:12 and notes on 6:18a and 17:23–27).

The LORD was merciful to them (v. 16). Illustrative of the Spirit's sovereign application of saving grace, the angels compelled them to leave doomed house and city and provided impenetrable escort through the vicious neighborhood.

This disaster will overtake me (v. 19). Unbelief mingled with faith in Lot. He feared the looming firestorm would catch him in unprotected terrain. The paradise-like plain he had opted for (13:10, 11) still attracted him on the day it was being turned into a Gehenna (vv. 24, 25, 28; cf. Rev 20:10). For his wife, perhaps a native of the plain, it was a fatal attraction (v. 26)—a sobering lesson for all who vacillate in the presence of the day of the Son of Man (cf. Luke 17:28–37; 2 Pet 2:6).

The LORD rained down burning sulphur (v. 24). Whatever role was played by local deposits of sulphur and bitumen (cf. 14:10), the precise timing and extent of the destruction in accordance with God's prophetic word evidenced his divine knowledge and power.

The entire plain (v. 25). Cf. 14:3 and note on 14:8.

---

16. Again, see *The Structure of Biblical Authority*, 154–71.

God remembered Abraham (v. 29) by saving Lot from the destruction of the wicked—the point of Abraham's circuitous intercession (18:23–32; cf. note on 8:1). The Judge of all the earth does right, not treating the righteous and the wicked alike (cf. 18:25).

19:30–38 ▷ The theme of Lot's separation from Abraham is resumed from 13:10–13.
Moab (v. 37) ... **Ben-Ammi** (v. 38). Like Ishmael, Lot's sons were born of the flesh, indeed of incest, and were the ancestors of future enemies of God's people. The fact that Abraham's nephew had (rejected) children before the birth of his heir would intensify his awareness of the delay in the fulfillment of God's promise (cf. 36:31).

Success and Dedication (20:1–21:34)

This section begins and closes with references to Abraham's sojourning in the land of the Philistines (20:1; 21:34) and his dealings with Abimelech. Its earlier counterpart, 13:18–14:24 (see the Introduction), celebrated God's power as Lord of heaven and earth to give victory in battle over the world forces and recorded Abraham's dedication of the spoils to him. Here God is exalted as Lord of life and death who closes and opens wombs (cf. 20:17, 18 and 21:1, 2), and Abraham consecrates to him the son of promise (21:4). The highlight is the birth of the heir (21:1–7), whose inheritance Abraham ensures by dismissing Ishmael (21:8–21) and whose peaceful existence in Canaan is secured by political treaty (21:22–34).

20:1–18 ▷ **Stayed in Gerar** (v. 1). The verb, indicating resident alien status, and the place name sound similar.[17] The pun emphasizes Abraham's lifelong pilgrim condition.

---

17. Heb. *g-w-r*, "stay (as a resident alien)"; *gĕrār*, "Gerar."

Sent for Sarah (v. 2). The time is between God's promise of Sarah's imminent pregnancy (18:10–14) and the birth (21:1, 2). Her rejuvenation is remarkable enough to revive the attractive-wife problem of earlier years (cf. 12:11–13; 20:13), and Abraham resorts to his old strategy. The humor of the situation fits the motif of laughter attending God's gifts of the heir (17:17; 18:12; 21:6, 7).

God came to Abimelech (v. 3). Though the Lord's protection of Abraham involved afflicting the king's household, as he had the Pharaoh's previously (cf. 12:17), the two episodes are quite different. The vouchsafing of the dream-revelation to the king and the nature of his response (vv. 4ff.) suggest the possibility that, unlike Pharaoh, Abimelech was a God-fearer, in spite of Abraham's apprehensions (v. 11).

Will you destroy an innocent nation? (v. 4). Abimelech's appeal was like Abraham's for Lot (18:23ff.) and led to the offer of the effective intercession of prophet Abraham for the king (v. 7; cf. note on 18:17). Abraham's role of intercessor-deliverer in the Sodom and Gerar episodes (cf. 20:17, 18) adumbrated the future mediation of blessing to all nations through his promised seed.

My land is before you (v. 15). Abimelech's offer recalls Abraham's generosity to Lot (cf. 13:9). In Abraham's experiences in both Gerar and Egypt (cf. 12:19, 20), divine intervention brought unexpected enrichment out of a dreaded situation of deadly peril (20:14–16; cf. 12:16), so that God's servants might learn to trust him to perform his impossible promise of salvation (cf. Matt 19:26; Mark 10:27; Luke 18:27).

God healed (v. 17). It was by his supernatural closing and revivifying of the wombs of the king's wives that the Lord most convincingly manifested to Sarah and Abraham the omnipotence that would bring life from their deadness, as promised. Sarah's rejuvenation, already in evidence, would surely bear fruit in the impossible birth of Isaac.

21:1-7 ▷ **What he had promised** (v. 1). The climactic event of the birth of the heir, so long anticipated, is simply narrated in poetic parallelism (cf. 1:27; 2:2). The nativity came at the time foretold in the heavenly annunciation (v. 2; cf. 18:10-14).

Circumcised him (v. 4). Isaac was consigned by oath under the authority and judgment of the Lord, separated unto holy status in a covenant that offered resurrection-vindication through faith-identification with Abraham's greater Son in his circumcision-crucifixion (cf. note on 17:11).[18]

God has brought me laughter (v. 6). By the gift of Isaac-Laughter, God made Sarah the mother of the covenant nation (cf. Isa 51:2) and ultimately of Jesus, the joy of all the earth. The way was now open for the realization of the covenant promises in their fullness, type and antitype.

21:8-21 ▷ The theme here is making the full inheritance secure for Isaac.

Mocking (v. 9). This verb is the one used in the name "Isaac";[19] the laughter attending Isaac's birth continues, but Ishmael's is malicious. Paul interprets it as a persecution of the son of promise (Gal 4:28f.).

Get rid of ... her son (v. 10). What Sarah demanded would quash any legal claim the servant woman's son might have on a portion of the estate.

Through Isaac ... your offspring will be reckoned (v. 12). Paul cites this as proof that the promised seed was not (at the higher level of fulfillment) the literal seed *per se*, but the elect (Rom 9:7). Otherwise, the unbelief and rejection of

---

18. See *By Oath Consigned*, 8, 44-47.
19. Heb. *ṣ-ḥ-q*. In the *qal*, this verb means "to laugh"; in the *piel* (the stem used here), the verb means "to play" or "to make sport." A *piel* form of this verb is also used in 26:8; see p. 94 footnote 2.

Ishmael (and numerous other Abrahamites afterward) would have constituted a failure of the Lord to bestow everlasting blessing on Abraham's seed, as he had promised.

Because he is your offspring (v. 13). In response to Abraham's natural fatherly concern for Ishmael as his (literal) son (cf. v. 11), the Lord promised for Ishmael, in his separation from the redemptive kingdom, the common grace blessings of earthly nationhood (cf. 17:20). This same prospect of nomadic nationhood for Ishmael was presented to Hagar by the Angel of God (v. 18; cf. 16:10–12). For the fulfillment, see 25:13–18. Yet what does it profit if one gain this transient world but suffer eternal loss? Ishmael's marriage to an Egyptian and his settling in the Sinai peninsula (v. 21) sealed his absorption into the world that would oppose Israel's attainment of the promised kingdom. Abraham's promptness in obeying the Lord's directive to give up Ishmael (v. 14) anticipated his similar obedience in the ultimate trial of faith, the demand that he deliver up Isaac on the altar (22:1ff.).

21:22–34 ▷ The narrative of Abraham's stay in Abimelech's territory is resumed (cf. 20:1ff.), possibly at a point prior to the events reported in 21:1–21.

God is with you (v. 22). Like King Melchizedek (cf. 14:19, 20), King Abimelech recognized Abraham as recipient of God's covenant blessing (cf. 20:6ff.).

The two men made a treaty (v. 27). Though a resident alien, the patriarch's economic-military stature was such that local kings found it expedient to enter into political treaties with him (cf. 14:13; 23:6). Ratification of the treaty involved the customary oaths (vv. 23, 24, 31) and witnesses (vv. 27–30). Abraham's God was the divine Witness invoked by both parties (vv. 22, 23, 31).

Accept these seven lambs (v. 30). As one special feature of the treaty arrangement, Abimelech recognized Abraham's proprietorship of a disputed well (vv. 25, 26) within his sphere of influence, giving public witness thereto by acceptance of the seven lambs set apart from the rest of the ceremonial animals (vv. 28, 29).

Planted a tamarisk tree (v. 33). Trees are associated with altars, natural symbols of the overshadowing divine presence (cf. 12:6, 7; 13:18). Here Isaac built an altar (26:25) and Jacob offered sacrifices (46:1).

Called upon . . . the eternal God (v. 33). Though the treaty with Abimelech expressed the present necessity of rendering unto Caesar what was his, establishing the cultus of the Lord here testified to the Lord's ultimate claim on this land and his purpose to take possession of it for Abraham's seed. Until the day of judgment, the patriarchs must accommodate themselves to the common grace civil magistrates, but the Abraham-Abimelech concordat did at least provide for a stable and prosperous life in Canaan for Abraham's heir (cf. v. 34 and 26:1ff.).

God's Oath of Confirmation (22:1–19)

22:1–19 ▷ Like the parallel section, 15:1–20 (see the Introduction), this passage records a divine oath in response to Abraham's obedient faith and an act foreshadowing Calvary.

God tested Abraham (v. 1). Abraham, like Christ, would become surety of blessing for others by obedience in a special trial.

Take your son . . . sacrifice him (v. 2). To offer up beloved Isaac, sole son of promise (cf. 21:12), tested Abraham's love of his Lord and his faith in him as the Almighty, who could restore Isaac from the dead (cf. Heb 11:19) so that the line of messianic hope might continue. Like Adam's special test (2:17), Abraham's involved a command exceptional to the pattern of God's regulations. God's demand for Isaac's life signified that the lives of all sons of fallen Adam are forfeit to God's justice.

Burnt offering (v. 2). Burnt offerings symbolized atonement, on the basis of which the offerer was consecrated to God (cf. Lev 1:3–9). In the role of sacrifice, Isaac would prefigure the passion of Jesus, as he obediently carried the wood to his Golgatha (v. 6) and on that wood of his altar was cut off (v. 9) in a total circumcision, a type of the crucifixion, by which the new covenant was "cut" (cf. Col 1:22; 2:11). But how could slain Isaac then be consecrated alive unto God? Abraham did not let that dilemma deter him: **he took the knife to slay his son** (v. 10). In effect, he performed a double typological role, like God the Son rendering the crucial obedience (cf. note on v. 1) and like God the Father offering his only begotten.

The Angel of the Lord (v. 11). The One who intervened was the pre-incarnate Son, only begotten of the Father, who must one day become the true sacrifice for sin and who, though slain, would rise again, consecrated forevermore in living priestly service (cf. Rev 1:17).

The ram ... instead of his son (v. 13). The substituted ram prefigured Christ as vicarious sacrifice (cf. Mark 10:45). Taken together with the Gen 15 oath of God, this episode was a divine commitment to the way of the cross of Christ. Sinners who by faith in him undergo death-judgment in him rise with him in living consecration to God. There was the answer to Abraham's dilemma.

On the mountain of the Lord it will be provided (v. 14b; cf. vv. 8 and 14a), or (the Lord) will appear. The name Moriah is based on this verb,[20] used again in the account of Solomon's building the temple at this site (2 Chr 3:1), identified there as the place where the Lord appeared to David (cf. 2 Sam 24:16, 17).

---

20. Heb. *r-ʾ-h*, "(*qal*) to see; (*niphal*) to appear."

I swear by myself (v. 15). The covenant promises were renewed (vv. 17, 18) as an oath (cf. notes on 15:17–21; Heb 6:13–18). One new detail is the figure of the sand; another, the more explicit indication that the kingdom-land would be gained through holy war (cf. note on 15:16). Typical fulfillment of this occurred under Joshua; the antitypical fulfillment will be executed by Jesus, returning in the glory of final judgment.

Because you have done this (v. 15) **. . . because you have obeyed me** (v. 18). It is by the obedience of Christ that the blessings of the eternal kingdom are secured for Abraham's innumerable seed of promise, Jews and gentiles elect in Christ (cf. Rom 5:19). It was on the grounds of Abraham's obedience that the typological, old covenant kingdom was secured for his numerous offspring who constituted the national election of Israel (see notes on v. 1 and 26:5).

Conclusion: Genealogical Succession (22:20–25:11)

A transition is made here from the patriarchal headship of Abraham to that of Isaac (cf. 25:19–35:29). Along with accounts of the deaths of Sarah (23:1ff.) and Abraham (25:7ff.) are narratives that focus on their successors. Rebekah's family background (22:20–24) and her marriage to Isaac (24:1–67) are dealt with; also, the dismissal of other children of Abraham (25:1–6), which left Isaac as the sole heir and undisputed covenant patriarch at Abraham's death (25:7–11).

22:20–24 ▷ Terah's name stood in the heading to this division of Genesis (11:27–25:11), for both the patriarchal and matriarchal roots of the covenant family were traceable to him (see note on 11:27). The record of Terah's more immediate descendants given in 11:27–30 is here resumed and carried another two generations to Rebekah, a descendant of both

Abraham's brothers, Haran and Nahor, the latter having married the former's daughter Milcah (v. 20; cf. 11:29), who bore him Bethuel, father of Rebekah (v. 23). Likewise, in the next generation, Leah and Rachel, wives of Jacob, were descended from both the Terahite lines collateral to Abraham, being daughters of Rebekah's brother Laban.

23:1–20 ▷ In the narrative of Sarah's death, the theme of the promised land becomes conspicuous again (cf. note on 16:1–16). In fact, the brief statement of her death (vv. 1, 2) serves as an introduction to what is actually a narrative about the acquisition of a burial ground for the covenant family in the land promised but not yet possessed (vv. 3–20).

So I can bury my dead (v. 4). In this hour, Abraham became acutely conscious of the postponement of the land inheritance (see notes on 15:13–16) as he confronted the lack of a burial place—a need that he had to meet immediately. Purchase of this family plot would be a witness to the Canaanite occupants of the land, expressing Abraham's faith that the Lord would by redemptive judgment at last make the alien family the triumphant possessors of their promised inheritance. It was a confession of faith, like the erection of altars in the Lord's name.

You are a mighty prince (literally, prince of God) **among us** (v. 6). On the Canaanites' recognition that the Abrahamic community was God's special protectorate, see note on 21:22.

The **Hittites** (v. 3) approached by Abraham were one of the early complex of peoples in the land (cf. 10:15; 15:20); their precise relation to the Hittites of the great Anatolian empire some centuries later is uncertain.

The cave of Machpelah (v. 9). That Abraham must secure the property by normal purchase procedures (v. 4) in the customary legal setting for such transactions at the city gate (v. 10) and using the official currency of local commerce (v. 16) shows again that the patriarchal age was one of common grace, pilgrim politics, not yet the time for a typological intrusion of holy kingdom judgment in Canaan.[21] But Abraham's obligation to honor, for the time being, the temporal authorities was further emphasized by the particular issue on which the bargaining apparently turned. If principles of later Hittite real estate law obtained here, Abraham's desire to isolate for purchase the cave at the end of Ephron's field (v. 9) and Ephron's counter-insistence on selling the entire field (v. 11) find ready explanation: the civil dues attaching to land ownership were transferred to a purchaser only if he obtained the entire unit.

So Ephron's field . . . was deeded to Abraham (vv. 17, 18). Hence, in the very act of expressing his faith that this whole land was his by divine promise, Abraham incurred new civil obligations requiring public acknowledgment of the present jurisdiction of other magistrates.

As a burial site (v. 20). Later buried here were Abraham (25:9), Isaac and Rebekah, and Jacob and Leah (49:31; 50:13).

24:1–9 ▷ Apart from the concluding summary notice of Abraham's final disposition and death (25:1–11), this is our last look at the patriarch. It reveals him in his old age, firm in his faith in the Lord who had been faithful to him and **blessed him in every way** (v. 1). Of most importance, God had provided the elect heir of the covenant promises. To this theme of the patriarchal succession the narrative here returns, relating Abraham's faithful attendance to his responsibility to secure for Isaac a wife suitable in terms of the revealed purposes of the covenant.

Put your hand under my thigh (v. 2; cf. v. 9). This oath gesture probably referred to the curse symbolized by circumcision.

---

21. *Kingdom Prologue*, 356–60; *The Structure of Biblical Authority*, 154–71.

Not ... from the Canaanites ... but ... my own relatives (vv. 3, 4). Terah's household would retain something of the faith of the living God transmitted in the Shem-Eber line, even though sadly compromised (cf. Josh 24:2, 14 and the spiritual circumstances reflected in Gen 29–31). Further, the Lord was to give Canaan to his people supernaturally in a redemptive judgment on the Canaanites; hence the Abrahamites were not to try to secure their hold on the land as a work of the flesh through intermarriage with the Canaanites. That would be a failure of faith akin to the futile scheme that resulted in Ishmael, the rejected son of the bondwoman.

Do not take my son back there (v. 6). Temporary sojourns in other lands made necessary by circumstances like famine were one thing, but a voluntary departure from Canaan to take up permanent residence elsewhere would be a repudiation of the hope and inheritance of the covenant promises. This would particularly be true of a return to Abraham's original country, from which the Lord had specifically separated him (cf. v. 7).

He will send his angel before you (v. 7). This affirmation of faith was a preview of the sequel (vv. 10ff.), in which the Lord by his sovereign providence honored Abraham's prophetic testimony.

24:10–27 ▷ **The servant ... set out for ... the town of Nahor** (v. 10). If the servant was Eliezer of Damascus (cf. 15:2), his journey led through his former country. The destination is apparently Haran (cf. 11:31; 27:43; 28:10), though there was a town named Nahor in the vicinity of Haran and Ur (cf. note on 11:28).

By this I will know (v. 14). A request for a sign was appropriate in that historical context of special revelation in direct connection with the life of the messianic family. The godly servant was, like his master, confident of the special superintending presence of God's Angel in this mission (cf. v. 7).

The one you have chosen (v. 14). Divine election, disclosed by special revelation, figured in the selection of Rebekah out of the Terah-Nahor household to be an ancestress in the line of Israel as distinctly as it did in the elective call of Abraham out of this same background to be the father of Israel.

Daughter of Bethuel (v. 15; cf. v. 24). See note on 22:20–24. Rebekah's identification of herself as of Abraham's kindred (v. 24) confirmed the evidence of the appointed sign (cf. vv. 4, 47) and prompted the preliminary presentation of gifts in recognition of her as the destined bride (v. 22).

The LORD has led me (v. 27). This verb,[22] within Genesis used only in this context (cf. v. 48), elsewhere describes God's special guidance of his people through the wilderness to the promised land by the Angel of the Presence and the Glory-cloud (cf. Exod 13:17, 21; 15:13; 32:34; Deut 32:12; Neh 9:12, 19; Pss 77:20; 78:14, 53).[23] At times the imagery is explicitly that of shepherding a flock (e.g., Ps 77:20; cf. Pss 23:3; 78:72). In contrast to the spectacular divine presence that led Israel in the age of the kingdom's advent, the Angel in the patriarchal age did not appear with the insignia of glory, or was not even visible, as in his guidance of Abraham's servant (cf. 16:7, 9; 19:1; 22:11, 15; 28:12; 31:11; 32:1; 48:16). But blessed were they who did not see, yet believed (cf. John 20:29). This godly servant was a visible proof of the presence of the invisible Spirit, mightily at work among men in transforming power, supernaturally bringing life into the spiritually dead, as well as out of dead wombs. Brought into the covenant by being brought into Abraham's household (cf. 17:12, 13, 23, 27), this man of faith

---

22. Heb. *n-ḥ-h*.
23. *Kingdom Prologue*, 369–72; *Images of the Spirit*, 17.

from outside the chosen genealogy had become a spiritual son of Abraham. He may not have qualified as the promised patriarchal son (cf. 15:3, 4), but he was of the promised seed of Abraham in the Gal 3:7 sense, an earnest of the numerous gentiles who, brought by the Spirit to faith in Abraham's messianic seed, would become the children of Abraham, the fulfillment of the promise that all nations would be blessed through him (Gal 3:8, 9, 29).

24:28–61 ▷ **A brother named Laban** (v. 29). The subordination of Bethuel (cf. v. 50), while the bride's brother, in cooperation with the mother (cf. vv. 28, 55ff.), made the marriage arrangements, reflects adoption of the fratriarchal type of family government. Laban's motives were not unmixed (cf. vv. 30, 36), though his consent to the proposal was couched in pious terms (v. 50; cf. v. 31).

He bowed down . . . before the LORD (v. 52). The servant's vital life of faith was expressed in repeated private and public acknowledgments of the Lord as the granter of success in this mission (cf. vv. 26, 48, 56).

They blessed Rebekah (v. 60). This farewell recalls the terms of the blessings promised the Abrahamites by God (cf. 22:17) and represented a step on the way to their realization.

24:62–66 ▷ The servant's report to Abraham concerning his mission is omitted. The narrative simply records the outcome: Rebekah assumed the place Sarah had occupied as wife of the covenant patriarch. From this point Isaac was the active head, though Abraham lived another thirty-five years.

25:1–11 ▷ **Another wife** (v. 1). Since Keturah is called a "concubine" (1 Chr 1:32; cf. v. 6), this relationship probably belonged to a time before Sarah's death. Inclusion of a notice of these descendants of Abraham was a desideratum, and the conclusion of the Abraham cycle was the most appropriate place for it. Here it subserves the major theme of the rejection of all the other sons of Abraham in favor of the son of promise (v. 6). Isaac thus stands at Abraham's death (cf. v. 11) as undisputed patriarchal successor and heir of the covenant inheritance (v. 5), with Rebekah, his divinely selected and provided wife (cf. 24:27).

Abraham ... died (v. 8). His pilgrimage from Haran to Machpelah lasted a hundred years (cf. 12:4 and 25:7).

He was gathered to his people (v. 8). This expression refers to a sequel to death (cf. Deut 32:50) and is not burial (compare 49:33 and 50:1–13). It reflects belief in the continued existence of the dead in the intermediate state. Abraham died in faith, still a stranger on earth but seeing from afar his heavenly country and the promised city of God (cf. Heb 11:10, 13–16 and see note on 23:4).

DIVISION SEVEN

Dismissal from the Covenant (Ishmael) (25:12–18)

Rejected Line of Ishmael (25:12–18)

25:12–18 ▷ This is the seventh division of Genesis. According to the regular pattern, the non-elect line of Ishmael is dealt with before chosen Isaac's family (25:19ff.). Like the record of the departure of Keturah's sons (see note on 25:1), this genealogy of Ishmael serves to dismiss Ishmael from the context of the Abrahamic Covenant (at least, until its new covenant stage), leaving the premessianic future of that covenant to Isaac and his descendants. This seventh division and the ninth (concerning Esau), though like the first and fourth divisions in treating the non-elect line, do not have the general, universal scope of the latter.

The twelve tribal rulers (v. 16). This development of the Ishmaelites into a twelve-tribe confederation formally similar to that of the Israelites was the fulfillment of God's promise to Abraham (see notes on 21:13ff.).

DIVISION EIGHT

Isaac, Covenant Patriarch (25:19–35:29)

Jacob's Election as Successor (25:19–27:40)

Jacob's Struggle for the Birthright (25:19–34)

25:19 ▷ **The account of Isaac.** This eighth division (25:19–35:29) covers the period of Isaac's active headship from his marriage in his fortieth year to his death (35:28, 29; see note on 24:62–66). The story now revolves around the selection of Isaac's successor, Jacob, and the birth of his twelve sons, from whom came the tribes of Israel. The tenth division of the book of Genesis covers the time when Jacob was the active patriarch, but here in the eighth division Jacob's life under Isaac's headship is traced, first in the land of Canaan (25:19–27:40), then out of the land in Paddan-Aram (27:41–33:17), and finally back in the promised land with his family (33:18–35:29).

25:19–27:40 ▷ The presence of Abraham's two sons, one by Sarah and one by Hagar, had given occasion for an exercise of divine choice. Another occasion for an even clearer demonstration that salvation is of the Lord was afforded by the birth to Isaac of twin sons. The principle of grace as opposed to human works was expressed in the patriarchal appointments of both Isaac and Jacob. In the former, the emphasis was on the sovereignty of God's power in effecting salvation; in the latter, on the sovereignty of God's good pleasure and purpose. This section begins (25:19ff.) and closes (26:34ff.) with the struggle of Jacob and Esau for the patriarchal succession. In between (26:1–33) is a description of the prosperous life of Isaac in the land of Canaan and the confirming of the covenant promises to him—a picture of what was at stake in the contention between Isaac's sons.

25:19–26 ▷ **Because she was barren** (v. 21). This feature, which reappeared in the experience of each of the three patriarchs (cf. 11:30; 29:31), served to bring out repeatedly the inadequacy of human resources for the achievement of the covenant promises, thus leading to prayer for God's supernatural intervention (cf. Isa 54:1ff.).

Inquire of the LORD (v. 22). The prenatal omen of the future struggle prompted further prayer to the Lord, probably at a patriarchal altar site. Rebekah needed reassurance concerning the outcome of the pregnancy.

The older will serve the younger (v. 23; cf. 9:25–27; Rom 9:12, 13). Paul points to this pre-birth oracle of God's elective love for Jacob in preference to his twin Esau as the decisive proof that election to salvation is sovereign and does not find its explanation in the natural situation, whether ethnic descent or human works (Rom 9:10–13). Indeed, it is strictly an act of mercy in spite of the ill desert of the elect (Rom 9:14–16). In Jacob's case, it was also in contravention of the customary right of primogeniture (cf. 1 Cor 1:27–29; Luke 15:1, 2).

Grasping Esau's heel (v. 26). This birth circumstance led to the name Jacob,[1] suggestive of the misguided efforts of this

---

1. In Hebrew, the name Jacob (*yaʻăqōb*) puns on the word "heel" (*ʻāqēb*).

younger son to secure the coveted position by his own devices. His life would demonstrate that human works are futile for the attainment of salvation and that covenant blessing is the sovereign gift of God's grace. Jacob would learn that the sinner's wrestling is not with man but with the Lord (cf. Hos 12:3, 4).

25:27-34 ▷ **Isaac . . . loved Esau** (v. 27). The sovereignty of God's love for Jacob and his hatred of Esau (cf. Mal 1:2, 3) was evidenced by its contradicting not only the convention of primogeniture but also the personal preferences of the one with authority to transmit the desired office.

Sell me your birthright (v. 31). This involved a double inheritance share and, in this family, the covenant succession and promises, all of which would be officially conveyed by Isaac's testamentary blessing (cf. 27:1ff.). Jacob's seeking to purchase by works the gift of grace betrayed his need of conversion to the way of faith.

Esau despised his birthright (v. 34). He was profane, an apostate from the covenant faith (Heb 12:16, 17; cf. Num 15:31).

Blessings for Isaac in Canaan (26:1-33)

Some foretaste of the nation Israel's enjoyment of the promised land was given in the life of Isaac. An account of this covenant blessedness is inserted here in the midst of the narratives of the rivalry of Jacob and Esau respecting it. The account includes two divine revelations confirming the promises to Isaac and his descendants (vv. 2-5 and 23, 24) and, between these, two incidents illustrating God's protective, prospering care of Isaac in difficult situations (vv. 7-11 and 12-22). It closes with a picture of Isaac securely settled in peaceful treaty relations with his neighbors (vv. 26-33).

26:1-6 ▷ **Live in the land** (v. 2). The famine (v. 1) was one of a series of situations encountered by Isaac similar to problems Abraham had faced. But in contrast to Abraham's recourse to Egypt for famine relief, Isaac was to discover the sufficiency of the Lord to preserve and even prosper him there in the land of want (cf. Ps 37:3, 4, 18, 19). Such prosperity is not guaranteed to all God's people at all times. It goes with possession of the kingdom, of which the Lord was pleased to grant Isaac a special prophetic earnest.

I will be with you (v. 3), a fresh form of the promise of God's covenant favor and help (cf. vv. 24, 28; 21:20, 22; 28:15). In renewing the promises of kingdom land and people and of mediation of blessing to all nations, the Lord identified them as his oath commitments to Abraham (vv. 3, 4).

Because Abraham obeyed me (v. 5). Reception of the covenant grant was a reward for Abraham's exemplary obedience, whereby he became a surety of the promised kingdom (on the old covenant level, not heaven itself) for Isaac and all his descendants (cf. v. 24 and see notes on 22:18).

26:7–11 ▷ The Lord impressed on Isaac that the covenant was being transmitted from Abraham to him (cf. vv. 2–5) by leading him through experiences of deliverance from difficulty strikingly like those of Abraham.

She is my sister (v. 7). In the stories passed down in the family circle, Isaac had learned of the incidents of Gen 12:10ff. and 20:1ff. The king of Gerar might possibly be the same one Abraham dealt with, but Abimelech was a Philistine dynastic title.

Looked down from a window (v. 8). Through the sovereign providence of the One who was with Isaac (cf. v. 3), resolution of the problem concerning Rebekah came through a chance glance.

Caressing his wife (v. 8). The verb[2] puns on Isaac's name.

---

2. Heb. *měṣaḥēq* (a *piel* form of *ṣ-ḥ-q*). See p. 77 footnote 19.

26:12-22 ▷ See 21:22ff. for Abraham's similar contention over wells with the Philistines and the ensuing peace treaty with the king (cf. 26:26ff.).

Planted crops (v. 12). Isaac's farming of the land accents the picture of firmly rooted settlement (cf. vv. 2, 3).

Because the Lord blessed him (v. 12). Famine (cf. v. 1) yielded to hundredfold crops (v. 12) and enormous wealth (vv. 13, 14). Here was the covenant secret of blessing for young Jacob to learn from the life of his father: trust in the all-sufficient Lord of grace, Immanuel. But Jacob experimented with salvation by human works (cf. 25:29ff. and 27:5ff.) and had to learn the hard way (cf. 27:41ff.).

Too powerful for us (v. 16). Cf. Exod 1:9. Envy incited by the evidence of God's favor on Isaac (cf. v. 28) induced antagonistic acts, depriving his community of vital water resources (vv. 15, 18) and driving them away from Gerar (v. 16).

The Lord has given us room (v. 22). Isaac's patient refraining from resort to anything but reliance on the Lord (vv. 19-21) resulted in even more firmly grounded prosperity.

26:23-33 ▷ This section describes Isaac's stay in Beersheba, somewhat further removed from Gerar and Philistine pressures. It concludes the account of Isaac's life in Canaan with notes on his covenants with the Lord and with King Abimelech.

The Lord appeared to him (v. 24). Isaac's preview experience of the promised kingdom included the cultic realities of divine presence and self-disclosure as well as a sampling of its cultural benefits. The promise to make Isaac's family a divine protectorate, given on the arrival at Gerar (vv. 2-5), was repeated in the face of the Philistine hostility that had meanwhile developed. Like Abraham's, Isaac's acknowledgment was an altar claiming the kingdom land for his Lord (v. 25; see notes on 12:7, 8; 22:33).

Let us make a treaty (v. 28). The Lord turns the hearts of kings according to his pleasure. Illustratively, this episode finds the Philistine king and his royal staff belatedly convinced that the Lord's purpose to bless Isaac was irresistible, and now resigned to proposing a mutual nonaggression pact. The nature of covenants as oath-bound commitments is clear in this transaction (vv. 28, 31). By this covenant Isaac's hold was solidified on the living space the Lord had opened for him in the land (cf. v. 22).

We've found water (v. 32). A fitting final note in this pastorale, prophetic of paradise found again.

Jacob's Reception of Isaac's Blessing (26:34–27:40)

After the interlude on Isaac's blessed life in the land, the narrative returns to the theme of the Jacob-Esau struggle. References to Esau's failings (26:34) and failure (27:30–40) enclose the account of Jacob's successful quest for Isaac's blessing (27:1–29). The implementation of the prenatal decree (25:23) was underway.

26:34, 35 ▷ The theme of Esau's profane disregard for the covenant is resumed from 25:34. He had despised its benefits; now he scorned its obligations by ignoring its requirement for godly, monogamous marriage. (See also note on 24:3, 4.)

27:1–29 ▷ **My blessing** (v. 4). Though Isaac lived over forty more years (cf. 35:28), he was 137 and judged a final testament timely. He presumably knew that Esau had bartered away his primogeniture rights (cf. 25:33; 27:36), but was prepared to make the legal disposition by which the blessings of the birthright would be formally conveyed to his favorite (25:28), the actual firstborn. And Esau was evidently willing to renege on his sworn commitment to Isaac.

That he may give you his blessing (v. 10). Rebekah remembered the prenatal announcement of the supremacy of the younger son and was also probably aware that Jacob had purchased the birthright, but in the face of the arrangements already afoot to bless Esau, she felt it necessary to resort to a deceptive stratagem to wrest the blessing for her favorite. Jacob himself deemed it necessary to fall in with his mother's counsel (vv. 11ff.) rather than appeal to the earlier bargain of the brothers. Like all Jacob's attempts to win the covenant heritage by his own efforts, that bargain was proving to be an empty victory.

The LORD your God gave me success (v. 20). Jacob put his finger on the secret of true success that he would be long in learning. His statement here is no expression of faith but an improper invoking of God's name.

So he blessed him (v. 23). The rite of blessing consisted of acts of identification (v. 24), invigoration (v. 25), imposition of hands (v. 26; cf. 48:13-20), and inspiration for the actual words of blessing (v. 27). See note on 28:4. Isaac's legal pronouncement was informed by divine inspiration and so constituted an irrevocable prophetic decree (cf. v. 33), a word of faith (cf. Heb 11:20). The blessings included paradisaical heritage (vv. 27, 28; cf. Deut 33:28); lordship over Esau, and indeed universal dominion (v. 29a; cf. v. 37; 49:10; Dan 7:27); and a protectorate relationship to God ensuring success in executing divine judgment and mediating blessing (v. 29b; cf. Gen 12:3; Num 24:3-9; Deut 33:26-29). Full realization of all these blessings of the Abrahamic Covenant would be attained only through the messianic descendant of Jacob, the true Israel, in the antitypical kingdom of the new kingdom.

27:30-40 ▷ **Rightly named Jacob** (v. 36). See note to 25:26. Esau's complaint against Jacob betrayed his own duplicity in being ready to accept Isaac's blessing after transferring the birthright by oath to his younger brother.

I have made him lord over you (v. 37). In spite of all the machinations of men, God had brought it to pass that the patriarchal headship had been irrevocably given to the younger twin, in fulfillment of the prenatal decree. Esau's tears of chagrin could not change this (cf. Heb 12:17). They evoked only a blessing that consigned his Edomite descendants to an infertile land, struggling, with but occasional success, to be independent of Israel's domination (vv. 39, 40).

EXILE ORIGIN OF THE TRIBAL FATHERS (27:41-33:17)

In the larger perspective of the history of the nation Israel, the significance of this section lies in its account of the origins of the twelve tribes in the birth of Jacob's twelve sons. This is placed in the middle (29:1-31:55) of the concentric pattern of this section. On either side of the center are Jacob's encounters with the Lord at Bethel (28:10-22) and Peniel (32:1-32). In terms of the life history of Jacob as chronicled in the seventh division of Genesis, this section covers the period of his sojourn outside the land of promise, from his flight from his antagonized brother (27:41-28:9) to his return home, Esau now reconciled (33:1-17). It is the period in which Jacob was transformed into Israel, the wrestler with God.

Jacob's Flight from the Land (27:41-28:9)

27:41-28:9 ▷ All the striving of Jacob and his mother left him miles away from actual enjoyment of the covenant heritage. The failure of his own devices was a schoolmaster to compel Jacob to the grace of God. Disappointment was the lot of Rebekah too.

Shall I lose both of you in one day? (27:45). Actually, that was precisely the unhappy consequence of her new scheme to help her favorite. Instead of losing Jacob as a murder victim (and Esau as a murderer), Rebekah lost all further contact with Jacob, for the sojourn far from home that she arranged extended beyond her lifetime (cf. 28:5). And Esau also left for other regions (cf. 28:9).

Do not marry a Canaanite woman (28:1). Whatever Rebekah's motivation and personal frustration, her scheming did prompt Isaac to take measures that would secure the proper development of the covenant family (see notes on 24:3, 4; 26:34).

The blessing of Abraham (28:4). Isaac's testamentary blessing (27:27–29) had been particularly concerned with the determination of the patriarchal succession. This farewell blessing, while confirming the earlier choice, elaborated on the specific promises of the Abrahamic Covenant that constituted the patriarchal inheritance (cf. Gen 17:1–8). Both blessings are prayers even while they are authoritative prophetic pronouncements, for it is God who imparts the blessing as a personal act—the words do not embody an impersonal magical potency. The laying on of hands in some acts of blessing (cf. note on 27:26) signified a communication of the substance of the blessing, an empowering, in particular, with the Spirit (cf. Deut 34:9 and note the equivalence of the promise of God's presence with blessing, e.g., in 26:3, 24). Such blessing acts are akin to anointing, and thus are typological of Christ's anointing his church with the Spirit, who is ultimately the promise of the covenant, the blessing of Abraham.

Esau . . . went to Ishmael (28:9). Jacob's departure did not alter Esau's rejected status, which was given further expression in his identification through marriage with the dismissed line of Ishmael.

Encounter with God's Angel at Bethel (28:10–22)

28:10–22 ▷ **A dream** (v. 12). This mode of revelation was suited to the state of Jacob's spiritual development.

The **staircase** (v. 12), a link between heaven and earth, represented the mountain of God, originally seen in Eden and renewed in Zion.[3] It was the cosmic axis and cultic focus of the kingdom, the place of God's enthronement amid the angelic hosts.[4] Jesus promised Nathanael such an opening of heaven when he identified himself as the true way by which man has access to God and saving help comes to man (John 1:47–51).

I will give you (v. 13). Jacob, like the builders of the ziggurat staircase at Babel (cf. 11:4), had been seeking to scale the heavens through human genius, but here he discovered that the heavenly presence descends with help for the helpless as a surprise gift of grace. Confirming Isaac's blessing, the Lord renewed to Jacob the promises of land, numerous descendants, and the mediation of blessing to all the earth (vv. 13, 14).

I am with you (v. 15). Before the kingdom comes, the personal presence of God, with his ascending-descending angel ministers (cf. Heb 1:14), is already the portion of the heirs of salvation.

Until I have done (v. 15). The success of Jacob's eventual homecoming from his exile-journey would be the success of the Lord, his guardian.

House of God . . . gate of heaven (v. 17). As the site of theophany and the staircase access to heaven, this place was God's temple and the door to his presence. Jesus, the true staircase, is also the true temple and door-gate (John 2:19–21; 10:7, 9; Rev 21:22).

Poured oil on top of it (v. 18), an act of consecration (cf. Exod 30:25–29). The pillar memorialized God's sanctifying

---

3. *Kingdom Prologue*, 375; *God, Heaven and Har Magedon*, 43–48.
4. *Kingdom Prologue*, 49.

of this place and prophesied that he would one day make all Canaan his holy land, site of his cosmic mountain, Zion.

Jacob made a vow (v. 20). In response to the Lord's promise to be his God (cf. 17:7), shepherding him safely back to the promised land (v. 21), Jacob pledged to make tributary confession of him (v. 22; cf. 14:20; 35:7, 14). At Bethel, Jacob began to become Israel.

Conflict with Laban (29:1–30)

The narrative of the birth of the tribal fathers (29:31–30:24) is preceded (29:1–30) and followed (30:25–31:55) by accounts of Jacob's conflict with his uncle, and father-in-law, Laban, which is finally settled by a covenant. Conspicuous in Jacob's acquiring of his wives, as in his acquisition of the patriarchal succession, was the element of deception—but with Jacob now the victim. And again it was the sovereign purpose of God, faithful to his covenant, that prevailed in and through all human scheming and striving, and in spite of Jacob's weakness.

29:1–19 ▷ Abraham's servant arrived with an impressive caravan (24:10ff.); Jacob, as a lone fugitive (v. 1). But there were remarkable similarities too, such as the meeting of the bride-to-be at the well (vv. 2–11), a plain token of God's special providential direction. The Lord was keeping his Bethel promise (cf. 28:15).

He . . . rolled the stone away (v. 10), a notable feat calculated to catch Rachel's eye and to impress Laban with the kind of service he could render. Rachel ran to Laban, and Laban came running to Jacob (vv. 12, 13).

My bone and my flesh (v. 14), a formula used in adoption texts. This, together with the absence of mention of sons of Laban until later, has led to the (disputed) suggestion that Jacob became Laban's heir by adoption.

Your wages (v. 15). Under a show of generosity, Laban reduced Jacob to a hired hand and exploited Jacob's love for Rachel to elicit a labor contract very favorable to himself (vv. 16-19)—tactics reminiscent of Jacob's own manipulating of Esau (cf. 25:29ff.).

29:20-30 ▷ This section on the acquisition of the wives opens (v. 20) and closes (v. 30) with references to seven-year periods of labor forced on Jacob. Laban contrived to make him work double the agreed time for beloved Rachel (v. 27). For the oppressive nature of working for Laban, see 31:6f., 38ff.

There was Leah (v. 25). Laban's duping of Jacob recalls Jacob's deception of Isaac (cf. 27:8ff.). Customary primogeniture rights were again a major factor (v. 26).

Zilpah (v. 24) and **Bilhah** (v. 29). Ancient texts attest the giving of maidservants as part of a dowry. This detail is included here because four tribes of Israel would derive from them.

Birth of Jacob's Sons (29:31-30:24)

The birth of the tribal fathers begins the transition from the three patriarchs to the twelve-tribe nation of Israel. Born outside of Canaan, they must repeat Abraham's migration from Paddan-Aram to the promised land. Their entry into Canaan, like later Israel's, would be a victorious return home. The account of their births continues the main theological emphases of the preceding narratives: the covenanted salvation is bestowed as a gift of divine grace in spite of human contrariness and as a miracle of divine power, not an achievement of human cunning.

29:31-35 ▷ The origin of the tribal fathers was in a polygamous situation amid family jealousies and strife; God's blessing was not based on virtues he found here.

Leah was not loved (v. 31). By granting unloved Leah sons first (vv. 32–35), and ultimately half of the twelve (cf. vv. 17–20), including the royal-messianic line of Judah and the priestly line of Levi, the Lord showed that natural human advantages are not the key to success in his kingdom.

30:1–13 ▷ As the narrative treats the sons of each woman in turn, the chronological sequence is disrupted.

Rachel was not bearing Jacob any children (v. 1). Rachel's barrenness was already mentioned at the outset of this section (29:31; cf. notes on 11:30; 25:21).

Am I in the place of God (v. 2). Jacob's exasperated retort reveals that he was discovering the failure of human works and was being driven to the way of faith.

She can bear children for me (v. 3). It was a custom, recognized in ancient law, for a barren wife to procure children as Rachel proposed. Authority over such children belonged to the wife (cf. 16:1).

Stopped having children (v. 9; cf. 29:35). To underscore further that the promised covenant future depended totally on the sovereign giving of God, the problem of barrenness arose in Leah's experience too (cf. vv. 17ff.). She had recourse to the same custom as Rachel had (v. 9), and together the two servant women bore four of Jacob's sons.

30:14–24 ▷ The contrast between the principles of faith and the works of the flesh reached its climax in the story of the origins of the twelve sons of Jacob with Rachel's resorting to the magical superstition of the aphrodisiac properties of the mandrake (vv. 14–16). Her frantic effort proved a total failure for her, while it was the occasion for her rival to be blessed with two more sons (vv. 16–20), and subsequently a daughter (v. 21; cf. 34:1ff.).

God listened to Leah (v. 17). Not magic but the God who answers prayer was the true source of the coveted blessing, as Leah acknowledged when naming her sons (vv. 18, 20).

God remembered Rachel (v. 22). The gift of new life was given not to Rachel the beautiful favorite of her husband but to Rachel the barren, who turned to God out of her hopelessness (vv. 22, 23). On remembering and covenant promise, see note on 8:1, and on God's mindfulness of a woman of humble estate, cf. Luke 1:48.

Pact with Laban (30:25–31:55)

The theme of Jacob's struggle with Laban is resumed (cf. 29:1–30). They matched wits in negotiating a further labor contract, which through God's blessing resulted in Jacob's acquiring great wealth in addition to his ample family (30:25–43). Then Jacob's household managed, again only through divine intervention, to escape from under Laban's domination, the terms of the separation being sealed by a covenant (31:1–55).

30:25-43 ▷ **Send me on my way** (v. 25). Jacob had the wife he came for (cf. 28:2) and much more. Moreover, his inheritance through Isaac awaited him in Canaan, and enough time had elapsed for Esau's anger to abate (cf. 27:44, 45). However, his service contracts apparently left within Laban's authority the granting of independent proprietorship to Jacob over whatever he had acquired from Laban's household (cf. 31:43; Exod 21:2ff.). Jacob's appeal to God's prospering of Laban through his own presence inflamed Laban's avarice rather than gratitude; he was adamant in denying the request (vv. 27–30). The arrangement for continued service that Jacob was compelled to propose was calculated to make the outcome definitely a matter of the providential control of the God whose favor he was assured of. The One who made Jacob's barren wives conceive sons would be able to order births of the sheep and goats in his favor, against all statistics increasing the sports in the flock, which were his wages (vv. 31–34). Jacob's employment of the technique of prenatal conditioning by visual impressions (vv. 37–42) need not indicate a relapse from reliance on the Lord, but recognition of his own responsible role. Certainly he attributed the outstanding success of the enterprise (v. 43) to the Lord's special intervention (cf. 31:9–12).

31:1–55 ▷ Jacob's exodus from his house of bondage paralleled Israel's exodus from Egypt under Moses in many ways (cf. Deut 26:5–8; Hos 12:12, 13). It involved Jacob's persuasion of his family to follow his leadership (vv. 4–16) and his confrontation with the oppressive master (vv. 23–42). Jacob led his family forth in response to God's call (v. 3). Their destination was the land of promise (vv. 13, 17). They spoiled Laban's household of wealth and gods (vv. 17–21). In their escape they were pursued and overtaken by Laban's superior forces (vv. 22, 23) and delivered by special divine intervention (v. 24). The episode concluded with a covenant recognizing Jacob's rights in the heritage of Abraham (vv. 43–55).

31:1–21 ▷ The account of the flight from Laban's household includes God's call to Jacob (vv. 1–3), Jacob's conspiring with his wives (vv. 4–16), and the actual departure (vv. 17–21).

Go back to the land (v. 3). God's summons to return coincided with Jacob's desire to get away from the intensifying hostility of Laban's sons, angered by their diminishing inheritance (vv. 1, 2; cf. Exod 1:9, 10). Jacob's call was like Abraham's to leave this same idolatrous household and head for Canaan.

I will be with you (v. 3). This recalls the Bethel promise (28:15; cf. Exod 3:12).

Your father has cheated me (v. 6). Jacob's complaint against Laban, stated briefly here, is expanded in the subsequent confrontation with Laban himself (vv. 38, 41; cf. Exod 1:11ff.). Here his argument for his escape plan emphasizes his relationship to God: **the God of my father has been with me** (v. 5). God had protected him (v. 7), blessed his breeding techniques (v. 8; cf. vv. 10ff.), and so enriched him at Laban's expense (v. 9). Jacob's ultimate appeal is that God, in keeping with their covenanting at Bethel, had commanded him to leave: **Go back to your native land** (v. 13). Rachel and Leah consented, adding their own complaint, in language reflecting ancient marriage contracts, that Laban was defrauding them (vv. 14–16). Jacob's strategy included a good head start for the plodding exodus caravan of family, livestock, and goods (cf. Exod 12:37, 38), the spoil of twenty years' conflict (cf. Exod 10:26; 11:2).

Headed for . . . Gilead (v. 21). This intermediate point on the way to Canaan, where Laban overtook them (v. 22), was some three hundred miles distant.

31:22–55 ▷ The account of Laban's pursuit includes God's warning to Laban (vv. 22–24), Jacob's controversy with Laban (vv. 25–42), and the concluding of a covenant (vv. 43–55).

God came . . . in a dream (v. 24). Laban's swift pursuit overtook Jacob's company short of Canaan in the region east of the Jordan (vv. 22, 23; cf. Exod 14:5ff.). But the threat of hostile action was defused by God's direct intervention, directing Laban not to enforce any legal claims against Jacob (cf. Exod 13:21f.; 14:19f.). Laban acknowledged that he was restrained by God's warning from exercising his superior power to seize any persons or goods. He pressed only the matter of his missing household gods (v. 30; cf. v. 19; 35:2). The episode of his futile search for them and Rachel's disrespectful treatment of them (vv. 31–35) points up the difference between the Lord God, who controls the whole situation, directing and delivering Jacob, and these idols, who can do nothing for Laban but must themselves be protected by Rachel (cf. Exod 12:12). Laban's failure to establish his charge opened the way for an impassioned counterattack by Jacob, a defense of his own conduct and a scathing exposure of Laban's meanness (vv. 36–42). There were ancient laws protecting herdsmen from the specific abuses Jacob complained of. His climactic conclusion was an acknowledgment of the decisive help of the **God of Abraham and Fear of Isaac** (v. 42).

Let's make a covenant (v. 44). Though still brazenly maintaining the legality of his position (v. 43), Laban was obliged to leave all in Jacob's possession and to settle for a mutual nonaggression pact. As seen in the ratification rituals here (vv. 45–54), covenants were essentially oath-bound commitments with divine witness and sanctioning.[5] Other characteristic features were the witness stones, which in this instance became in effect a boundary marker on Israel's eastern border, and the meal (vv. 46, 54) sealing the covenant, which in this case did not produce a bond of unity but established a separating barrier (v. 52). Jacob's sacrifice (v. 54) was a ritual confession that the Lord had been his Provider-Protector, and a provisional fulfillment of his Bethel vow (cf. 28:21, 22).

Encounter with God's Angel at Peniel (32:1–32)

Corresponding to Jacob's vision of the Lord and the angels on his flight from Esau (cf. 28:10–22) was a similar encounter as he returned to Canaan and Esau (now in nearby Seir). His meeting with God happened unexpectedly amid his preparations for the meeting with Esau, leaving the latter as an anticlimax. This section begins (vv. 1, 2) and closes (vv. 22–32) with the angelic and divine visitations. In between, Jacob's

---

5. *Kingdom Prologue*, 1–4.

preparations for meeting Esau are narrated, with his prayer for God's help in the center (vv. 9–12), bracketed by two accounts of defensive tactics he employed (vv. 3–8 and vv. 13–21).

32:1, 2 ▷ **Angels of God met him** (v. 1), evidence again of that constant special presence of God promised at Bethel (28:12, 15; cf. 31:3, 10), not always visible but nonetheless there (cf. 2 Kgs 6:17).

Mahanaim (v. 2), "two camps," recalled the revelation of the presence of a second, angelic company above, a heavenly shield and escort for Jacob's company below.

32:3–21 ▷ Apprehensive of the inevitable meeting with Esau, Jacob planned to placate him by a show of deference in the initial negotiations (vv. 3–8). At the news that Esau was approaching with a force of retainers larger than Abraham led to battle against the coalition of eastern kings (v. 6; cf. 14:14), Jacob took steps to save at least half his company from the impending attack (vv. 7, 8).

Save me, I pray (v. 11). The spiritual transformation under way in Jacob was voiced in this prayer, expressive of personal unworthiness (v. 10) and dependence on the Lord. The basis of his plea in the present crisis was God's previous revelation to him, the recent promise of assistance on his return to Canaan (v. 9; cf. 31:3; 28:15), and the Bethel renewal of the Abrahamic promise of numerous descendants (v. 12; cf. 28:14). If Esau were to annihilate his family, where was this promised future (vv. 11f.)? Jacob confessed God's covenant-keeping hitherto: because the second company, i.e., God's angels (cf. vv. 1, 2), has been with him, Jacob, the sole fugitive, has become a family of two companies (v. 10; cf. v. 7). Jacob's adoption of the supplementary measure of an advance appeasement gift need not signify a quick lapse from the faith expressed in his prayer. His expectation would be that the Lord would prosper his responsible action, turning the heart of Esau to accept the gift, as he had prevailed upon Laban to forbear from his hostile intentions (cf. 31:42).

32:22–32 ▷ Before the anticipated, ominous meeting with Esau, an unanticipated, omen-laden meeting with God occurred. Jacob's prayer (vv. 9–12) had been, in effect, an unplanned preparation of soul for the unexpected. By the river Jabbok on the boundary of the promised land (cf. Num 21:24), Jacob must undergo a judicial ordeal prior to passing over, as the nation Israel later did in its passage of Jordan and entry into Canaan.[6] This was the climactic disclosure to Jacob that attainment of the kingdom offered in redemptive covenant was a matter of prevailing with God, not outwitting or overpowering human rivals. The salvation for which he prayed (cf. v. 11) was ultimately from God's wrath, not Esau's.

A man wrestled with him (v. 24). The Angel of the Lord, captain of the angelic hosts of Bethel's staircase to heaven (cf. vv. 1, 2; 28:13; Josh 5:13f.; Hos 12:3), engaged Jacob that night in wrestling combat, a form of judicial ordeal attested in ancient lawsuits.[7] Could Jacob the grasping sinner wrest from the holy God a verdict of justification? That was the real issue all along. It was by faith in the Lord who appeared to him in the darkness, committing himself to the way of the cross, that Abraham had been accounted righteous (cf. notes on Gen 15). So too Jacob, enabled by the grace of the Angel-Adversary, prevailed by supplicating faith (vv. 25, 26; cf. Hos 12:4).

Touched the socket of Jacob's hip (v. 25). Smiting Jacob at the seat of his reproductive powers portended the suffering of Jacob's messianic seed (none other than his ordeal Opponent, here pre-incarnate). He would be smitten of God (Isa 53:4)

---

6. "Trial by Ordeal," 86.
7. "Trial by Ordeal," 88.

to win justification for Jacob and all the promised seed of Abraham. As in the Gen 15 and 22 oath episodes, the messianic Angel was here prophetically committing himself to the judicial ordeal of Golgotha.

Your name ... Israel (v. 28). His new name registered his conversion to the way of faith in the God of grace. It pronounced the blessing-verdict: justified by faith (cf. Gen 15:6). The name Israel also identified the Adversary as El, God (cf. v. 29). Jacob echoed this identification in naming the site Peniel,[8] to commemorate the mercy that spared his life in the face-to-face encounter with his heavenly Judge (v. 30).

Jacob's Return to the Land (33:1–17)

33:1–17 ▷ The chapters of the Paddan-Aram period (27:41–33:17) come full circle with the record of Jacob's return to the promised land and to Esau. Long put off, the confrontation with Esau follows now as an anticlimax to the decisive surprise encounter with the Angel, its outcome made clear beforehand by the blessing Jacob secured at Peniel.

Bowed down ... seven times (v. 3; cf. vv. 6, 7). Isaac's blessing had proclaimed that others of Jacob's kindred (in particular, Esau and his line), as well as the nations, would bow down to him (cf. 27:29). That promise, signifying Jacob's election to the patriarchal succession (cf. 25:23), would be fulfilled in the history of Israel, the nation, and especially in the messianic scion of Israel (cf. 49:10). Meanwhile, Jacob found himself doing the bowing to Esau and so discovered afresh the emptiness of the apparent victories he had won earlier through his works of the flesh.

Like seeing the face of God (v. 10). At Peniel, Jacob saw God's face and his life was spared (32:30). Similarly, now he has seen the dreaded face of Esau (cf. 32:20) and has been fa-

---

8. Heb. *pĕnî'ēl*, "face of [*pĕnî*] God [*'ēl*]."

vorably received. Esau's reconciled countenance reflected the countenance of the Lord lifted up on Jacob in peace.

Esau accepted it (v. 11). This gift was not a further payment in the original, unscrupulous birthright transaction, but acceptance of it did serve to seal Esau's reconciliation to the situation.

Esau . . . back to Seir (v. 16; cf. 28:9). Esau left the inheritance in Jacob's undisputed possession.

Succoth (v. 17). About a decade elapsed between Jacob's exodus from Laban's house of bondage and the Shechem episode (cf. 34:1ff.), possibly much of it at Succoth between his Transjordan victory and his crossing of the Jordan into Canaan.

Israel in Canaan under Isaac (33:18–35:29)

Like the closing section (22:20–25:11) of the Abraham cycle in the sixth division of the book of Genesis, this final section of the eighth division traces a transition in the patriarchal headship, this time from Isaac to Jacob. It covers the period of Jacob back in Canaan with his sons until Isaac's death (see notes on 25:19). The narrative deals with the solidifying of Jacob's position as heir of the covenant promises of land and descendants; with actions of his sons significant for future leadership in the nation; and with genealogical matters, births, and deaths.

33:18–20 ▷ He arrived safely . . . in Canaan (v. 18). Jacob's entrance into Canaan and settlement there was "in peace" (NIV, "safely"), as stipulated in his Bethel vow (28:21). Purchase of ground (v. 19) expressed his confidence that his future lay here, according to God's promise.

Set up an altar (v. 20). Jacob followed in the steps of Abraham, who, on his arrival in Canaan, set up altars successively at Shechem and Bethel (see notes on 12:6, 8; cf. 35:7).

34:1–31 ▷ The future tribal heads displayed familiar failings of their father, particularly Jacob's impatient grasping for the promised inheritance by human means, especially deceit. Manifestly, their election, like Jacob's, was an unconditional act of divine mercy.

Dinah (v. 1) was some fourteen years old (cf. 30:21; 37:2).

The Hivite (v. 2), possibly an Achaean group.

Shechem's liaison with Dinah (v. 2) and the subsequent proposals of a merger of the peoples of Hamor and Jacob to resolve the ensuing tensions (vv. 3ff., 9ff., 16, 22) threatened to undo what Jacob's leaving Canaan to secure a wife had been intended to achieve (see notes on 24:3, 4 and 28:1).

Intermarry with us (v. 9). The terms Hamor suggested resembled arrangements made for Hittite merchants in foreign territory. The patriarchal household was to have a peaceful, common grace relationship with the peoples of Canaan, but not lose their distinctive covenantal-religious identity by becoming absorbed into them through intermarriage.

Jacob's sons replied deceitfully (v. 13). The role of Dinah's brothers in dealing with her abduction reflects fratriarchal practice in Laban's family. Their deceit copied Jacob's earlier behavior.

Become like us by circumcising all your males (v. 15). This was no missionary call to unite with the Lord's people, but rather an act of sacrilege, a reprehensible misuse of the holy covenant sign for the purpose of inflicting vengeance. The Shechemites shared in the profanation of circumcision, regarding it as a mere tribal convention and adopting it as a means to get wives and wealth (vv. 21–24). What it actually brought on them was the curse of the sword symbolized by circumcision (vv. 25, 26; cf. note on 17:11).

Killing every male (v. 25) . . . **taking as plunder everything** (v. 29). Vengeance belongs to the Lord, to be executed in his time. In the age of Moses, the Amorites were ripe for judgment (cf. note on 15:16), and God's people then were commissioned to holy war, to seize the land of Canaan and slay its inhabitants as a typological intrusion of the principle of final judgment. But the massacre of the Shechemites by Simeon and Levi in the common grace, patriarchal age of pilgrim politics was a faithless, outrageous deed. Jacob's reprobation of their cruel treachery (v. 30) was later expressed in what should have been a blessing on them (cf. 49:5–7). Such were the objects of God's elective grace whom he preserved (cf. 35:5) for a role in the future of the covenant nation (cf. 1 Cor 1:27–29).

35:1–15 ▷ **Go up to Bethel** (v. 1). The period of Jacob's Paddan-Aram sojourn began with the dream-theophany at Bethel, and now there remained a vow to be fulfilled there (cf. 28:22; 31:13). Return to Canaan (33:18) was not enough; Jacob must move on from Shechem to Bethel.

Jacob said to his household (v. 2). The patriarchal prophet relayed the divine directive. Since the covenant community is composed of household units, all in Jacob's household were subject to his covenantal discipline.[9] His demand that they purge themselves of the material tokens of idolatry brought from Laban's household (v. 4; cf. 31:19; Josh 24:24) was an enforcing of the covenant's primary requirement of exclusive allegiance to the Lord (cf. Exod 20:3–5).

God ... who has been with me (v. 3), a good confession of God's faithfulness to his Bethel promise (cf. 28:15) and a rebuke of the faithless impatience of Jacob's sons at Shechem.

The terror of God (v. 5). This divinely induced panic (cf. 32:1ff.; Exod 23:23, 27), which prevented pursuit and annihilating attack (cf. 34:30), confirmed the truth of Jacob's testimony concerning God's presence with his people (v. 3).

---

9. *Kingdom Prologue*, 367; *God, Heaven and Har Magedon*, 107.

The name **El Bethel** (v. 7) memorialized the divine revelation given there and marked Jacob's performance of his vow in the erection of an altar and the service of consecration (cf. vv. 14, 15). It was by their cultic life as an altar-congregation bearing the name of the Lord God that the patriarchal family avoided loss of their distinctiveness and absorption into the surrounding culture, even while maintaining peaceful, common grace relations with the Canaanites. In their altars they presented the ultimate claim of Yahweh on this land, without attempting to enforce that claim prematurely.[10]

God appeared to him again (v. 9; cf. 48:3, 4; Hos 12:4, 5), reiterating the change of name to Israel (v. 10; cf. 32:28) and renewing the Abrahamic Covenant promises of an assembly of nations as descendants, royal dynasty, and land (cf. Gen 17:6, 8; 28:3, 4, 13, 14).

35:16–29 ▷ The cycle concludes with a series of birth and death notices and a genealogical list.

Benjamin (v. 18). Since the main development in the history of Israel during the period covered in this eighth division of Genesis was the appearance of the twelve tribal fathers, it could not close without recording the birth of the twelfth son. Appropriately, too, it placed here at the end a summary of the twelve (cf. Matt 10:2–4; Rev 21:12–14). Also noted is an offense of Reuben, the firstborn (v. 22), that affected the course of future leadership in Israel (cf. Matt 10:4). In his final blessings, Jacob bypassed Reuben, Simeon, and Levi (49:3–7; cf. note on 34:30) and assigned royal supremacy to Judah (49:8–12). With Isaac's death (v. 29), the transfer of patriarchal headship to Jacob was completed. When the story is resumed in 37:1ff., it recapitulates, for Isaac lived over a decade after the sale of Joseph into Egypt.

---

10. *Kingdom Prologue*, 372–78; *God, Heaven and Har Magedon*, 108–9.

DIVISION NINE

DISMISSAL FROM THE COVENANT (ESAU) (36:1–37:1)

REJECTED LINE OF ESAU (36:1–37:1)

36:1–37:1 ▷ **The account of Esau** (36:1). Cf. notes on 25:12–18. Esau is identified as Edom, the national designation of his descendants (cf. 25:30). What was foretold about Esau in the prenatal announcement (25:22) and Isaac's blessing (27:39, 40) is seen coming to pass in this largely genealogical account (cf. 1 Chr 1:35–54). It is arranged, like the Jacob narratives, according to periods when Esau was in Canaan (vv. 2–5) or elsewhere (vv. 6–43). On his selection of wives (vv. 2, 3), see note on 26:34. Esau's decision that the land was too small for him and Jacob—hence his move to Seir, southeast of the Dead Sea (vv. 6–8)—might have been in anticipation of Jacob's return (cf. 32:3; 33:16). A secondary appearance of the heading formula in v. 9 (cf. v. 1) marks the move to Seir. The descendants' names in vv. 2–5 are repeated at the start of the list in vv. 10–14, just as the sons of Jacob summarized in 35:23–26 are listed again at Jacob's move to Egypt (cf. 46:8ff.). The list of political-military leaders in vv. 15–19, which includes names found in vv. 2–5 and 10–14, indicates a development of the family into a tribal organization.

Seir the Horite (36:20). Esau's descendants subjugated the earlier Horite population of Seir (cf. Deut 2:12) and intermarried with them. The names of Seir's descendants are also traced genealogically first (vv. 20–28) then listed as chiefs (vv. 29, 30).

Kings who reigned in Edom (36:31). These kings (vv. 31–39) were not a dynasty but were elected by the other chiefs.

Before any Israelite king reigned (36:31). Abraham's royal seed was the subject of promise, prophecy, and anticipatory legislation (cf. 17:6, 16; 49:10; Deut 17:14–20) but had not emerged by Moses' day, to which the Edomite kings are traced. A geographical-administrative classification of the chiefs is given in vv. 40–43.

Jacob lived . . . in Canaan (37:1). The ninth division closes with a transition to the following account of Jacob's family in the promised land. For similar closing transitions, see 4:25, 26; 6:8; 35:29.

DIVISION TEN

Jacob, Covenant Patriarch (37:2–50:26)

Family Disunion in Canaan (37:2–38:30)

37:2 ▷ The period of Jacob's patriarchal headship is treated in the tenth division of Genesis (37:2–50:26). This closing portion is designed as a transition to the book of Exodus. Its main historical theme is the descent of the house of Jacob into Egypt for their long sojourn in the land of Ham (cf. 15:13; Ps 105:23) until the time came for the exodus and triumphant return to the land of promise (cf. 15:14, 16; Ps 105:26ff.). Beneath the surface, the Spirit is revealed at work trying and transforming the fractious sons of Jacob into a covenant family more unified and honoring to the Lord. Chiastically arranged, the tenth division begins with Jacob in Canaan with his family (37:2–38:30) and closes with the family's returning of Jacob to Canaan for burial (47:28–50:26). Adjoining those terminal sections are accounts of Joseph in Egypt (39:1–41:57) and Jacob in Egypt (46:1–47:27), each an instance of God's prospering care of his people amid adversity. At the center is the story of two preliminary journeys of Jacob's sons to Egypt and back, which led to Jacob's decision to go there with his whole household (42:1–45:28). As the climactic speech of Joseph in 45:1–15 brings out, the history of Joseph and his brothers is one of God's sovereign accomplishing of his purpose of deliverance (cf. 45:7) by overruling and indeed working through the brothers' sinful acts. This history thus stands as a remarkable parable of the death of the Savior, nailed to the cross by wicked men as God had decided beforehand in his counsels of redemption (cf. Acts 2:23; 4:28).

37:2–38:30 ▷ Attention centers here on the beginnings of the dominance of the tribes of Joseph and Judah, the royal messianic line (cf. 1 Chr 5:1, 2). The focus is first on Joseph, who, by his remarkable attainment of international political eminence, became the active leader of the family during those days of Jacob's patriarchal headship and received the rights of the firstborn. In 37:2–36, Joseph's destined leadership is disclosed in dreams and its realization set in motion by his jealous brothers, in spite of themselves. Then the focus shifts to Judah. As the one whose tribe was to achieve preeminence in the long run, he receives particular notice, especially in the parallel terminal sections (here in ch. 38 and in 49:8–12) and in the central section (cf. chs. 43 and 44).

37:2–11 ▷ **Israel loved Joseph ... born to him in his old age** (v. 3), and after the long barrenness of Rachel, Jacob's favorite wife. Features of Isaac's family life reappear here: parental favoritism and contention for the birthright, with a younger son attaining it. The brothers saw in the gift of the special robe to Joseph Jacob's determination to give the birthright to him (cf. 48:8ff.; 1 Chr 5:1f.). On Reuben's forfeiture of it, cf. 35:22.

Joseph had a dream (v. 5). The heaven-sent dream, its certainty shown by its being doubled (cf. v. 9; 41:32), revealed Joseph's coming elevation over his brothers. The Lord's choice of Jacob over Esau, likewise revealed beforehand, had not coincided with Isaac's preference; but in Joseph's case, the parental favorite was confirmed by God's elective disclosure. The second dream foretold Joseph's eminence over even Jacob, within the Egyptian political context. That was compatible with Jacob's continuing covenantal-patriarchal headship. The working out of Joseph's dreams is the underlying story line of the whole tenth division.

Jealous of him (v. 11). The brothers' hatred, already aroused by Jacob's favoritism and by Joseph's reporting of their slothful management of the flocks (cf. vv. 2–9), was intensified by Joseph's reporting of his dreams (vv. 5, 8). They behaved like Cain, seed of Satan, obsessed by jealous hatred because of God's acceptance of his brother, with murderous thoughts crouching like a beast at his heart, ready to overmaster him (cf. 4:7). Joseph's brothers were prepared to yield to such demonic dominion rather than accept the rule of Joseph forecast in the dream (v. 8). The exposure of the dismal spiritual state of the covenant family at this early stage provides a foil for the dramatic improvement narrated in the following chapters.

37:12–36 ▷ Through uncharacteristic lack of foresighted planning, Jacob delivered his favorite into the clutches of the seething siblings (vv. 12–18). That they were herding in the Shechem area suggests the continued special protection of God over the patriarchal family of alien residents in Canaan (cf. 34:30). Unmindful of God's presence, intent only on how they were hidden out in the field from Jacob's eyes (cf. 4:8), they vented their fratriarchal hatred: **Let's kill him** (v. 20). Acceptance of Reuben's proposal (vv. 21, 22) would not mean sparing Joseph's life; indeed, dying in the pit would be a protracted agony. In their callous, merciless cruelty, they ignored their victim's pleas (vv. 23–25a; cf. 42:21). It was admitted in

Judah's suggestion to sell Joseph that the guilt of Joseph's death would still be on their hands even though leaving him in the cistern did not involve their shedding his blood (vv. 26, 27; cf. vv. 21, 22). Starting here, the narrative repeatedly directs attention to Judah, the ancestor of David and Jesus.

Ishmaelites (vv. 25, 28; cf. 39:1) possibly signifies here nomadic merchants (cf. Judg 8:24). Midianites, or Medanites, describes them ethnically (vv. 28, 36; cf. 25:2). The brothers show heartless disregard for their father, mocking his hope to give Joseph the firstborn benefits by presenting the tunic, sign of Jacob's purpose, as evidence of Joseph's death (vv. 31–35). Their wiles recalled Jacob's own earlier deception of his father (cf. esp. 27:15, 16).

Sold Joseph in Egypt (v. 36). Many Asiatic slaves were in Egypt, largely as a result of war but also through the commercial route. In 39:1 the Joseph narrative is resumed and with it the theme of the Israelites' sojourn in the Egyptian house of bondage, as Genesis sets the stage for Exodus.

38:1–30 ▷ The Bible's long-range concern with the genealogical origins and royal dynasty of the promised Messiah accounts for the sudden transfer of concentration to Judah and his relation to Tamar. At the same time, this narrative continues the emphasis of chapter 37 on the dissension and degeneration in Jacob's family during their residency in Canaan. Some two decades of family history are covered from the sale of Joseph to about the time of Jacob's departure to Egypt, before the narrative backs up to follow again the career of Joseph, now as a slave in Egypt (cf. 39:1ff.).

38:1–11 ▷ **Judah left his brothers and went down** (v. 1). Judah's descent from Hebron's heights to lowland Canaanite territory mirrored his spiritual declension. His departure resumes the theme of the tensions among the brothers.

Daughter of a Canaanite (v. 2). On the problem of intermarriage with the Canaanites, see note on 24:3, 4. As subsequent developments in Judah's family indicate (vv. 6ff.), such intermarriage, unchecked, would result in the corrupting of the covenant family and in their becoming partakers of the Canaanites' eventual doom (cf. vv. 7, 10). Genesis 38 thus contributes to the contextual theme of God's arranging, through the sale of Joseph (37:36 and 39:1), for Jacob's move to Egypt by showing the necessity of removing his family from Canaan.

Produce offspring for your brother (v. 8). Levirate marriage, widely practiced, was incorporated into the Mosaic legislation (cf. Deut 25:5ff.). The one who performed the levirate duty might suffer diminution of his own estate (v. 9; cf. Ruth 4:5, 6).

Live as a widow (v. 11). Judah denied Tamar her right, falsely blaming her for the deaths of Er and Onan instead of recognizing the evils his own foolish move had begotten.

38:12–30 ▷ Again, an episode of deception. When Jacob's pretense became obvious to Tamar (v. 14, cf. v. 11), she resorted to a ruse of her own to secure her levirate rights (vv. 14ff.).

Your seal and its cord (v. 18). Cylinder seals, worn on a cord about the neck, functioned as personal signatures.

Shrine prostitute (v. 21). This practice reflects the rottenness of Canaanite society and religion. The contaminating impact of these evil associations on Judah, evident in his flagrant moral lapses, underscores his need for conversion, which we see occurring in the sequel.

Bring her out (v. 24). While surreptitiously avoiding his paternal obligations to his daughter-in-law, Judah hypocritically asserted his authority to have her punished for her offense against the family. (For relevant Mosaic laws, cf. Lev 20:14; 21:9; Deut 22:20ff.)

More righteous than I (v. 26). A beginning of repentance and conversion surfaces in Judah's acknowledgment that his guilt in this affair was greater than Tamar's.

Perez (v. 29). As history turned out, the son and inheritance rights Tamar successfully contended for involved a place in the royal lineage of David and Jesus Christ (cf. Ruth 4:18–22; Matt 1:3; Luke 3:33). That our Lord descended from Tamar and the even less righteous Judah was congenial to his mission as one who did not come to call the righteous but sinners to repentance and forgiveness (Luke 3:32).

JOSEPH IN EGYPT
(39:1–41:57)

Psalm 105:16–22 recalls the present story of Joseph in Egypt as part of a rehearsal of God's wonderful acts (vv. 17–22), acts of covenant faithfulness (vv. 7–11) his people should proclaim among the nations (vv. 1–6). Psalm 105:23ff. conjoins a reference to Jacob's entrance into Egypt, the episode in Gen 46 and 47, the parallel section to the present chapters (cf. note on 37:2). It notes that God not only preserved but prospered Joseph and Israel in their perilous situation in Egypt, just as he had protected the patriarchs in Canaan (cf. vv. 12–15). "He sent a man before them" (v. 17) distills the significance of the developments in Gen 39–41. By sending a forerunner, and afterward the famine (cf. Ps 105:16), God was orchestrating the descent of Israel into Egypt, with a view to the ultimate goal of the exodus under Moses (cf. Ps 105:26ff.). This section of Genesis exhibits God's remarkable control of human affairs, ordering the most unlikely circumstances into an interlocking chain of events that move unerringly and astonishingly to the predestined outcome in fulfillment of his redemptive purpose.

39:1–6a ▷ On the chronological order, see note on 38:1–30.
The LORD was with Joseph (v. 2). Hence the slave was soon promoted to a position of high trust and authority in the house of the royal chief steward (vv. 3–6). Cf. Acts 7:9, 10. The Lord's sovereignty over all the world, in particular his ability to guard and bless his people away from the promised land as well as within it, had been similarly demonstrated in the lives of Abraham, Isaac, and Jacob. God's favor was so unmistakably the explanation of his servants' outstanding success that others, like Potiphar (v. 3), recognized this. Repeatedly, the presence of God's favored ones brought earthly benefits to others outside the covenant community (v. 5; cf. 30:27). All Egypt, with the surrounding nations, was to benefit from the wisdom God gave Joseph to deal with the famine (cf. 41:54–57). The promised extension of the covenant blessing of salvation to all the nations (cf. 12:2, 3) would, however, await the advent of the messianic seed of Abraham.

39:6b–23 ▷ In the wondrous web of divine providence, false accusation and imprisonment became the next step toward Joseph's political eminence in Egypt.
How then could I . . . sin against God? (v. 9). Joseph's insight into the nature of sin as primarily an offense against God (cf. Ps 51:4) and especially his steadfast adherence to the moral demands of the covenant (vv. 8–10) evidenced the powerful presence of the Holy Spirit, applying even in premessianic ages the sanctifying benefits of Christ's work of salvation.
His cloak in her hand (v. 12). Joseph's sale into slavery involved his brothers' use of his robe to deceive Jacob (37:10ff.; cf. 27:15). His imprisonment again involved a falsehood about a garment of his, this time to deceive Potiphar (vv. 13–18). Before long, another robe would figure in Joseph's advancement (cf. 41:42).

This Hebrew (v. 14; cf. v. 17). See notes on 10:21 and 14:13. In the Gen 39–Exod 10 context, location of many of the Old Testament occurrences of "Hebrew," this designation may carry (especially on the lips of Egyptians) the overtones of despised Asiatic foreigners (cf. 43:32) and refer to a broader group of Eberites than simply the family of Abraham.

In prison (v. 20). Joseph was still under Potiphar's jurisdiction here (cf. 40:3, 4).

The Lord was with him (v. 21). Chapter 39 ends as it began with Joseph unjustly suffering loss of freedom, yet continuing to enjoy the Lord's protecting, prospering blessing. The result once more was that under Potiphar's prison officer, as under Potiphar himself in his house, the whole sphere of Joseph's confinement was entrusted to his oversight (vv. 22, 23).

40:1–8a ▷ The closing of the prison doors on Joseph was designed by the Lord to be an opening of a door to the palace. The connection between prison and palace was established by the placing of two high palace officials in the prison where all was under Joseph's care (vv. 1–4). To do that, God turned Pharaoh's heart against these two courtiers (v. 2). Such sovereign control exercised over the Egyptian empire and monarch anticipated the Lord's later steering of Pharaoh, heart and hand, as he arranged for Israel's exodus deliverance.

We both had dreams (v. 8). This second pair of dreams (cf. 37:5–10) would prove the key to open the palace door. Absence of the professional dream interpreters usually available in the court created an opportunity for Joseph, whom the Spirit had given a special interpretive gift of wisdom (cf. Acts 6:10; 7:10).

40:8b–23 ▷ **Do not interpretations belong to God?** (v. 8b). Joseph held fast to the name of his God in boldly faithful witness (cf. 39:9; 41:16, 25, 28, 32).

Lift up your head (v. 13; cf. vv. 18, 20). This expression is used for both of the opposite fates forecast in the two dreams.

Remember me (v. 14). Confident of his interpretation, Joseph by faith grasped the providential opportunity to get his cause, a just one (cf. v. 15), presented to Pharaoh, who could overrule the captain of the guard and secure his release from prison. This request was to bear fruit in due course. Confirmed as a true prophetic spokesman of his God by the fulfillment of the dreams according to his interpretation (vv. 20–22), Joseph was, however, temporarily forgotten by his beneficiary, the chief cupbearer (v. 23). But there was a purpose in the delay: Pharaoh himself must become indebted to Joseph's wisdom so that he would not merely set him free but exalt him next to the throne in Egypt.

41:1–36 ▷ **Pharaoh had a dream** (v. 1). This third pair of dream-revelations (cf. v. 32 and note on 40:8) would bring Joseph to the lofty position where his own dreams of supremacy over his brothers came true.

The wise men of Egypt (v. 8). It was not the absence of Pharaoh's experts in divination this time but their failure that would provide Joseph with his opportunity. Moreover, his meeting with Pharaoh would now be a confrontation of the wisdom of God with that of Satan and the world.

Today I am reminded (v. 9). The similarity of Pharaoh's problem to his own revived the royal cupbearer's memory of Joseph and his obligation to him (vv. 9–13) so that he finally served the divine purpose as Joseph's way out of prison into the presence of Pharaoh (v. 14; cf. notes on 40:1–4). The situation here is much like that of Daniel in Nebuchadnezzar's court, with the series of wisdom contests pitting God's servants against the Babylonian wise men in tests of learning (Dan 1:17–20), interpreting of dreams (Dan 2:1ff.; 4:5ff.), and deciphering of enigmatic writing (Dan 5:5ff.). In both cases, the contests were calculated to manifest the power and wisdom of the living God of the covenant against the gods of the world powers. They also resulted in the honoring of God's witnesses.

God will give Pharaoh the answer (v. 16; cf. vv. 25, 28, 32). Joseph engaged in the wisdom ordeal forthrightly in the name of his God (cf. note on 40:8b). The account of Pharaoh's rehearsal of his dreams to Joseph (vv. 17-24) essentially repeats the previous one, with supplementation only of detail (cf. vv. 21, 24). Joseph's wisdom gift was displayed not only in his ability to explain Pharaoh's dreams (vv. 25-32) but in his administrative recommendations to meet the coming famine emergency disclosed in the dreams (vv. 33-36). In proposing measures for the relief of Egypt, Joseph showed the kind of concern God's people are to have for the general welfare of humanity in this common grace world (cf. Matt 5:43-48).[1] The testimony of Joseph to the Lord, God of salvation, would thereby be all the more commended to the unbelievers. Moreover, the provident policy he suggested would prove to be God's means of preserving the covenant family of Jacob in the famine crisis (cf. 42:1ff.).

41:37-45 ▷ **No one so ... wise as you** (v. 39). Joseph's proposal included the appointment of a capable administrator to supervise the program (v. 33), and Pharaoh recognized as the obvious choice the maker of the proposal, the one who had just defeated all the wise men of Egypt in the court wisdom contest (vv. 37, 38; cf. Ps 105:21, 22). Joseph's witness to God found a point of contact in the sense of deity in Pharaoh (cf. Rom 1:19ff.) and evoked at least a formal acknowledgment of God as the source of wisdom (vv. 38, 39).

In charge of the whole land of Egypt (v. 41; cf. v. 33). From slave to vizier of Egypt—astonishing, but a trifle to the

---

1. *God, Heaven and Har Magedon*, 104.

God who brings the promised seed from barren wombs and life from the dead. The Lord would later repeat such triumphs in the days of Israel's slavery in the land of Ham—in the rescue of the infant Moses from the Nile to be adopted into Pharaoh's household and in the subsequent prevailing of Moses in ordeals of wisdom and power against the court magicians. These were early intimations of the ultimate triumph of the messianic man child caught up from the cross and his ordeal with the dragon to the throne of God to rule all nations (cf. Rev 12:1–5).

Robes of fine linen (v. 42). In a traditional Egyptian installation investiture, Joseph received another robe (cf. 37:3). This one symbolized the authority before which Joseph's brothers would bow in fulfillment of his dreams (cf. 42:6ff.).

Daughter of Potiphera, priest of On (v. 45). Joseph's taking an Egyptian wife would not adversely affect the development of the covenant community as did the intermarriages that transpired back in Canaan (cf., e.g., Gen 38). Also, his clear-cut commitment to the worship of the Lord God would forestall misunderstanding of his marrying Potiphera's daughter as though it were a capitulation to Re, the sun god, whose cultic center was On.

41:46–57 ▷ The account of the two decades of Joseph's life in Egypt, separated from Jacob's family (Gen 39–41), concludes by describing his public administration during the seven years of abundance (vv. 46–49) and at the outset of the predicted famine (vv. 53–57). In between, the birth of his two sons is recorded (vv. 50–52). By virtue of Jacob's adoption of these two grandsons, they became tribal heads of the twelve-tribe nation of Israel and constituted for Joseph the double portion of the firstborn (cf. 48:8ff.). In Joseph's naming of his sons, he continued his witness to his God in the idolatrous environment of Egypt. The names Manasseh and Ephraim celebrated the providence of God that had totally overcome the consequences of his brothers' hatred, turning Egypt from a place of suffering into a land of blessing (vv. 51, 52).

All countries came to Egypt (v. 57). God had now sent both the forerunner and the famine (cf. Ps 105:16, 17), and the stage was set for the descent of the covenant community into Egypt.

Refining of the Covenant Family (42:1–45:28)

God put the tribal fathers of Israel through a trial, an assaying of their spiritual mettle. Out of it, Jacob's family emerged much refined, preserved by God as a surviving remnant to continue the covenant line and redemptive program. The famine was the arena of the divine testing, but the heat of the assaying-refining crucible was brought to the critical pitch by Joseph's testing of his brothers (42:15, 16; on the metallurgical image, cf. Pss 17:3; 66:10; 139:23; Jer 6:27; 11:20; 17:10; 1 Chr 29:17). In the brothers' intensifying trial, the scene alternated between their meetings with Jacob (42:1–5; 42:25–43:14; 45:16–28) and Joseph (42:6–24; 43:15–45:15), the two poles of their self-inflicted dilemma, to which they were driven relentlessly back and forth. In the process, the dreams of Joseph were fulfilled, Judah rose to leadership, family reconciliation was achieved, and the strange providence of Joseph's sale into Egypt was explained. God sovereignly designed that sin against Joseph as a means toward the immediate deliverance of the covenant family from the existence-threatening famine and toward the long-range objective of bringing them into Egypt in preparation for the exodus deliverance and the acquisition of the promised inheritance in remembrance of the covenant with Abraham.

42:1–5 ▷ In the family emergency, Jacob's patriarchal authority brought the brothers together for a united endeavor (vv. 1, 2).

Jacob did not send Benjamin, Joseph's brother (v. 4). How the brothers would relate to this new favorite of Jacob and treat their father himself would be the crucial point in the upcoming test, revealing whether there had been a change in the spiritual climate. Driven by famine from the land where they had hated Joseph unto death (v. 5), they might be troubled by the thought of the similar fate of the first murderer, driven from the land that refused its crops (cf. 4:11–14). Heading for Egypt, they would be mindful that this was the destination of the merchants to whom they sold Joseph (cf. 37:28).

42:6–24 ▷ **They bowed down to him** (v. 6). This literal fulfilling of Joseph's dream (v. 9) was repeated at the second meeting (cf. 43:26, 28; 44:14) and was underscored by frequent acknowledgments that the brothers and Jacob were servants of this Egyptian lord (cf. vv. 10ff.). After some twenty years, they might not have recognized their teenage brother in this august, culturally Egyptianized figure, speaking through an interpreter (v. 23), even had he not deliberately concealed his identity. Obliged by his strangely pointed probing to think and speak of Joseph and Benjamin (vv. 7–12; cf. 43:7; 44:19f.), the brothers too were concealing the facts about Joseph, particularly his identity as the victim of their hatred (v. 13). But their conscience was being further stirred.

You will be tested (v. 15). This verb, used in the Pentateuch only here (cf. v. 16), highlights the central theme of these chapters (cf. notes on 42:1–45:28). Joseph began to create a situation like that of their earlier crime against him and Jacob, with Benjamin now in his role (cf. note on 42:4), to see if the brothers had had a change of heart (vv. 15, 16).

Surely we are being punished (v. 21). Their sense of guilt had been intensified by the three days in confinement, disputing the disturbing turn of events (v. 17), and then by Joseph's posture as one who feared God (v. 18) and had regard for their starving family (v. 19)—a studied contrast to their own pitiless deafness to their brother's pleas from the pit (vv. 21, 22).

He had Simeon taken (v. 24). There was a remarkable correspondence between the individual measure of guilt of Reuben and Simeon in the sin against Joseph and the treatment meted out by the uncanny vizier.

42:25–43:14 ▷ This encounter of the brothers with Jacob unfolded in two meetings (42:29–38 and 43:1–14).

What is this that God has done to us? (42:28). The first meeting is introduced by an account of the further tactic Joseph used to heighten the brothers' sense of divine judgment pursuing them (42:25–28).

You have deprived me of my children (42:36). Jacob, from whom they were still hiding their sin against Joseph (cf. "one is no more," v. 32), must have startled them by this complaint, in which he spoke more accurately than he knew. Reuben, as the eldest and the one with a relatively clearer conscience (cf. 37:21ff.; 42:22), ventured a response to their agitated father (42:37). But to propose that in the event of Benjamin's loss Jacob be additionally deprived of two grandsons was not well calculated to console him or win his confidence (cf. 42:38). When the continued, mounting pressure of the famine forced a renewed meeting with Jacob (43:1, 2), it was Judah's proposal that prevailed. More reassuringly, he appealed to the preservation, not destruction, of the life of the family members (43:8) and offered, apparently, to forfeit his own inheritance interests in the family's future (43:9). This marked Judah's emerging leadership in the covenant history (cf. note on 37:26, 27). Jacob's previous experience in dealing with potentially hostile parties (cf. 32:13ff.) was reflected in his arranging a conciliatory gift for the man in Egypt (43:11–13).

God Almighty grant you mercy (43:14). Precisely the appropriate prayer. On this divine name, see note on 17:1.

43:15–45:15 ▷ The structure of this section is similar to that of the preceding one. The second and decisive encounter with Joseph, introduced by an account of the brothers' growing apprehension (43:15–25), took place in two separate meetings (43:26–34 and 44:1–45:15). Benjamin's presence (43:16) now made possible Joseph's ultimate test (see note on 42:15, 16). The brothers had become so disconcerted that overtures to a dinner invitation alarmed them (43:18ff.).

Your God and the God of your father (43:23). Even the astonishing assurances of the steward, reflecting Joseph's religious influence on him, and the warm display of hospitality could not calm them (43:24, 25). Their fears prompted prostrations in acknowledgment of Joseph's lordship (43:26–28), a further fulfillment of his dreams. The inexplicable correspondence between the seating of the eleven and their ages seemed a startling sign (43:33). By blatant favoritism for Benjamin (43:29, 34), Joseph probed for a betrayal of the old spirit of jealousy. But the final test called for Benjamin to be singled out not in favor but in mortal danger (44:1ff.).

He will die (44:9). By contriving to make Benjamin appear guilty of stealing his personal property, a sacred instrument of alleged divination, Joseph put him in jeopardy of a death penalty, as the brothers recognized (cf. 31:32). The sequence of the search (44:12; cf. note on 43:33) seemed to validate the claimed power of divination (cf. 44:15).

They threw themselves to the ground before him (44:14), a reversal of their roles when Joseph was at their mercy; **God has uncovered your servants' guilt** (44:16). Though spoken with reference to the present episode, this confession reflected their intensifying sense of guilt over the great sin of the past (cf. 42:21, 28).

Go back to your father in peace (44:17). Echoing his steward (cf. 44:10), Joseph insisted on punishing Benjamin alone and sending the others back to Jacob without his favorite—a reproduction of the old situation. Joseph's elaborate scheme had worked out to perfection.

Judah went up to him (44:18). Again, the leadership of Judah (cf. 44:16 and note on 43:8, 9).

Let your servant remain here as my lord's slave in place of the boy (44:33). The design of God's Spirit was also developing to perfection—in the hearts of the covenant family.[2] Judah's self-sacrificing offer, a striking parable of the mission of the Savior who would come from Judah's stock, was for Joseph an overwhelming demonstration of the change he was looking for (45:1, 2). Equally overwhelming for the brothers was Joseph's self-disclosure: **They were terrified at his presence** (45:3). Their guilt, long suppressed, would be long in yielding to an assurance of forgiveness (cf. 50:15).

It was to save lives that God sent me ahead of you (45:5; cf. 50:20). Joseph's interpretation of the divine providence in the immediate famine crisis suggests to the reader the larger truth that the events that brought Jacob's family into Egypt subserved God's historic program of redeeming a remnant people through Moses and Messiah. On this passage, see the note on 37:2.

You shall live in the region of Goshen (45:10). When Joseph originally interpreted Pharaoh's dreams, he appended practical counsel to save Egypt from the famine. Again, as he related that revelation to his brothers (45:6, 7), so disclosing that he had a prophetic gift from God and did not really divine from a silver cup (cf. 44:15), he immediately added a

---

2. *Kingdom Prologue*, 380–82.

practical plan to secure the welfare of the covenant community. Goshen in the East Delta area was near enough to the royal court for Joseph to exercise direct supervision, yet, being cattle country, it afforded a measure of isolation from the mainstream of Egyptian influences (cf. 46:31–34). Intermarriage with Egyptians would be minimized—and, of course, in Egypt the problem of intermarriage with Canaanites that had troubled the patriarchal family was left behind.

45:16–28 ▷ Joseph's directives were turned into a royal invitation (45:16–20). The attitudes of the pharaohs at the entrance and exodus of Israel is a study in opposites. Though Jacob's family entered Egypt to preserve their lives (cf. 45:7), God would later have to bring them out for the same reason. Joseph implemented Pharaoh's generous grant (45:21–24), sending the brothers back for the last in their series of meetings with Jacob (cf. notes on 42:1–45:28). He needed no longer fear a jealous reaction against Benjamin (45:22), but he did warn the ten not to fall into arguing about the long-hidden sin they would soon have to confess to their father (45:24). Judging from the account in 45:26, they accented the positive in their report to Jacob.

I will go (v. 28). The narrative from 39:1 on has pointed to this momentous decision. It concluded the period of Jacob's life in Canaan with his family (37:2ff.) and was a prelude to the four-century sojourn in Egypt (cf. Gen 15:13).

Jacob's Family in Egypt
(46:1–47:27)

The final phase of Jacob's life was with his family in the land of Egypt. The account is introduced by a last appearance of the Lord to Jacob (46:1–4). Then a genealogical listing of the small company that descended into Egypt (46:5–27) provides a foil for their subsequent great increase there (as noted in the closing summary in 47:27) and a linkage to the book of Exodus (cf. Exod 1:1–7 and 6:14ff.). The main subject in this section is Joseph's arranging for the settling of the covenant community in Egypt (46:28–47:12), with Jacob's blessing of Pharaoh the central highlight of the narrative (47:7–10). This is set in the context of Joseph's administration of the total Egyptian economy during the famine crisis (47:13–26; cf. 41:46–57), a theme resumed here from 39:1–41:57, the corresponding section in the chiastic tenth division of Genesis (cf. notes on 37:2).

46:1–4 ▷ On his way out of Canaan, Jacob resorted to the patriarchal border altar at Beersheba in testimony that this land belonged to his Lord and was his own heritage by divine grant of grace (46:1).

I will go down to Egypt with you (v. 4). In a final revelation to Jacob, the Lord gave reassurance that in leaving the land he was not leaving his heavenly Protector behind (cf. Isa 43:1–6). Indeed, the Egyptian sojourn would prove a step toward the fulfillment of the covenant promises, as Israel grew there under Joseph's oversight into a great nation in readiness for eventual return to Canaan (46:2–4).

46:5–27 ▷ A family catalogue is inserted at this epochal transition, the end of the era of the patriarchs in Canaan. (Cf. the genealogical list at the close of the period of Jacob's sojourn in Paddan-Aram [35:10–26].) It sets the present few in contrast to the promised ultimate nationhood (cf. v. 3; Exod 1:5, 6; Deut 10:22). Of course, there were more than seventy (46:27), that being a conventional total in this stylized genealogy (cf. notes on 5:1 and 11:10–26). In the sixty-six total in 46:26, apparently Jacob, Joseph, and his two sons are excluded. In Acts 7:14, Stephen follows the LXX tradition, which included five additional descendants. The heading in 46:8

must be understood to include some born after the settlement in Egypt (cf., e.g., 46:21), the design being to list the founders of the fathers' houses in Israel. (Cf. the parallel lists in Num 26 and 1 Chr 4–6.)

46:28–47:12 ▷ **Jacob sent Judah ahead** (46:28). Attention is again called to the emerging leadership of the ancestor of Israel's royal dynasty.

You are still alive (46:30). What father Jacob saw in the magnificent charioteer (46:29) was his long-lost son, alive from the dead. Joseph now put into operation the plan he had privately disclosed to his brothers (cf. 45:10, 11). He diplomatically arranged for Pharaoh to perceive the secluded location in Goshen, actually selected to preserve the Israelites from the influence of Egyptian religion, as one required by their occupation and dictated by consideration for Egyptian distaste for rearing livestock (46:31–47:6).

Jacob blessed Pharaoh (47:7, 10). The greater blesses the lesser (cf. Heb 7:7). The relation of Jacob and his covenant family to Pharaoh and Egypt was beneficial, particularly through the offices of Joseph. This contrasted with the later disaster inflicted on this empire through Moses when it cruelly oppressed God's people (Exod 12:32; cf. also Gen 13:17–20). Their immediate role as vehicle of blessing was illustrative of the Abrahamic Covenant's goal of blessing the gentiles through the messianic scion of Judah's line.

My pilgrimage (47:9). Jacob aptly depicted his life and the patriarchal period as a whole (cf. "the pilgrimage of my fathers," v. 9) as a sojourning in this world, a journeying in faith to the celestial city of promise (cf. Heb 11:9–16). The basic theme of this section is stated in the closing summary (47:11, 12): the settling of Jacob's household prosperously in Egypt through the agency of the man God had sent ahead of them (cf. notes on 39:1–41:57).

47:13–27 ▷ The record of Joseph's administrative handling of the twice-seven cycle of famine and plenty, begun in 41:46–57, is continued here. His policies benefited everybody concerned.

Egypt and Canaan (vv. 13, 14, 15). The people of the lands of promise and Israel's foreign sojourn were saved from starvation, as the Egyptians themselves gratefully acknowledged (47:25). Pharaoh benefited by the increase of his power in Egypt and the firmer establishment of his hegemony over Canaan (47:14–26).

And the Israelites . . . increased greatly (v. 27). Remarkably, the Israelites prospered beyond others around them. This closing note indicates that the process of fulfilling the divine promise given at the descent of Jacob's household of seventy (cf. 46:5–27) into Egypt (cf. 46:3) was quickly under way. The Israelites' prosperity and Pharaoh's increased power resulting from Joseph's actions are stressed here in anticipation of the crisis with which the book of Exodus begins. There, a pharaoh, ungratefully forgetful of Joseph (Exod 1:8; cf. Gen 40:23), cites the numerousness of the Israelites as an excuse for crushing them under his powerful hand. So a relation of mutual blessing became one of mutual cursing.

REUNION AND RESTORATION TO CANAAN (47:28–50:26)

As Genesis draws to a close with the covenant family in Egypt, everything points to the exodus event and the return to Canaan. The Jacob-Joseph relationship dominates the narrative. It begins (47:28–31) and ends (50:22–26) with oaths imposed by the father and son, respectively, stipulating their burial in the promised land. The centerpiece is the account of the great funeral procession to Canaan to bury Jacob there

(49:29–50:14), an earnest of the exodus. The tenth generations-division of Genesis (37:2–50:26), which began with Jacob's return to Canaan from Paddan-Aram, thus concludes with his return there from Egypt. On either side of the center of the present section (49:29–50:14) are records of the twelve tribal fathers, their present relationships, and their future prospects (48:1–49:28 and 50:15–21), each of these passages resuming and concluding narrative strands found in the corresponding first section (37:2–38:30) of this division (see note on 37:2). Continued here from the immediately preceding section (46:1–47:27) is the theme of blessing. The focus shifts here from the present blessing of the Egyptian world, particularly through Joseph, to prophetic blessings pronounced on the tribes of Israel (esp. 49:1–28), which would culminate in the mediation of blessing to the entire world through Christ, descendant of Judah.

47:28–31 ▷ **Bury me where they are buried** (v. 30). Among the instances of patriarchal faith celebrated in Heb 11 (see vv. 21, 22) are these oath transactions of Jacob and Joseph (cf. 50:22–26). Insistence on burial in Canaan was a staking of claim to a personal future share, beyond imminent death, in the promised kingdom of God (cf. Heb 11:13–16, 39). On the oath gesture in v. 29, cf. note on 24:2.

The time drew near for Israel to die (v. 29). Apparently this is the same occasion referred to in Gen 48. Hebrews 11:21 appends to its reference to the latter the conclusion of the former (47:31b). The burial of Jacob in Canaan was also enjoined upon Joseph's brothers (cf. 49:29–32), but he was approached first, as Jacob's trusted favorite and the one with the necessary official authority.

48:1–49:28 ▷ Through legal pronouncements, Jacob prophetically delineated the future unfolding of the Abrahamic promises. The earlier selection of Joseph for the double portion (cf. 37:3ff.) was implemented in the elevation of two of his sons to the status of tribal fathers, accomplished by Jacob's act of adoptive blessing (48:1–22). By a final testamentary disposition, the patriarch bestowed blessings on all his sons, ordering the places of the twelve tribes in covenant history (49:1–28).

48:1–22 ▷ The setting of imminent death (vv. 1, 2; cf. note on 47:29) gives to Jacob's blessings in Gen 48 and 49 a testamentary character.

God Almighty . . . blessed me (v. 3). It was the kingdom blessings of people and land promised in the Abrahamic Covenant, renewed in turn to Isaac and then, at Bethel, to Jacob (48:3, 4; cf. 28:13, 14; 35:11, 12), that Jacob was transmitting to the next generation. In blessing Joseph by blessing these two sons (cf. 48:15, 20), Jacob first declared his intention to adopt Ephraim and Manasseh (vv. 5–7), then performed the legal gesture (vv. 8–12), and finally confirmed the adoption through the words of blessing (vv. 13–20).

Reckoned as mine (v. 5). On these two grandsons was thus bestowed a status like that of Jacob's own sons. Joseph thereby received the double inheritance (cf. notes on 37:2–4), and so the name of his mother, Rachel, would be honorably memorialized, though it was Leah who was buried in the Machpelah cave (cf. v. 7; 49:31).

In the territory they inherit (v. 6). By faith Jacob regarded the promised land secured and proceeded to assign tribal allotments.

Israel's knees (v. 12). Jacob's receptive embrace of the two upon his knees (cf. v. 10), hardly literal since they were about twenty years old, probably was a legal rite for acknowledging one's children (cf. Gen 30:3; 50:23). Words of blessing then conveyed the adoption (v. 16). The similarity of the Hebrew words for knees and bless constitutes a wordplay—i.e., the legal gesture and verbal pronouncement said the same thing.³ This prophetic blessing supplements that in Gen 49, where Ephraim and Manasseh are not distinguished in the blessing on Joseph. In the giving of the greater future to the younger Ephraim (v. 19), God's sovereignty in bestowing covenant blessing again appears (cf. the similar cases of Jacob and Joseph; see also v. 22). Also evident again is the Spirit's mighty transformation of the covenant community, particularly Jacob-Israel. He confessed the divine Angel as his kinsman-redeemer and faithful shepherd in all his journeyings (vv. 15, 16). Jacob concluded by developing the opening theme of the superior land grant Joseph would enjoy after the conquest of the Amorites (vv. 21, 22).

49:1–28 ▷ Jacob's testamentary blessings here encompass all twelve sons, arranged according to the mothers: Leah's six (vv. 3–15); the handmaids' four (vv. 16–21); and Rachel's two (vv. 22–27). Cf. Deut 33:1ff.

In days to come (v. 1). This phrase points to the ultimate eschatological outcome; the prophecy extends into the messianic age. A shadow falls over the blessings of Reuben (vv. 3, 4) and of Simeon and Levi (vv. 5–7) because of their serious offenses (cf. 34:25ff.; 35:22).

Judah . . . your father's sons will bow down to you (v. 8) as they had to Joseph, but Judah's government would be that of God's kingdom.

The scepter will not depart from Judah (v. 10). By the Davidic Covenant (2 Sam 7:16; cf. notes on 17:6–8) kingship was guaranteed to Judah forever.

Until Shiloh comes (v. 10; see KJV). This name identifies Messiah as prince of peace (cf. Isa 9:6, 7). David's dynasty would culminate in Shiloh, and at that new covenant level his

---

3. Heb. *berek*, "knee"; *b-r-k*, "bless."

throne would become everlasting (cf. Matt 1:1; Luke 1:32, 33). On the NIV rendering "to whom it belongs," cf. Ezek 21:27.

The obedience of the nations is his (v. 10). Extending beyond David's reign over the tribes of Israel, Shiloh's dominion would be worldwide (cf. Ps 72:8–11; Isa 11:10); his peace would be proclaimed to the nations (cf. Zech 9:9, 10). Only through suffering would he attain glory; he would come riding the kind of donkey anciently used in death rites that ratified covenants (v. 11a; cf. Zech 9:9, 11), his garments stained with the blood that washes white the robes of God's people (v. 11b; cf. Rev 7:14; 19:13). Jacob's blessings on the others (vv. 13ff.) are briefer and refer to the old covenant tribal history. Joseph's blessing, however, is longer (vv. 22–26), agreeably to the greater prominence of the Joseph tribes, especially Ephraim. Tracing these blessings to their Source, Jacob confessed God as the almighty Shepherd and Rock of Israel (vv. 24, 25; cf. 48:15, 16; Deut 32:4) and with seasoned hope expressed a longing for the salvation promised in God's covenant with the fathers (v. 18).

49:29–50:14 ▷ This central passage of the final part of Genesis (see note on 47:28–50:26) is concentrically arranged: it begins (49:29–33) with the giving of the charge to bury Jacob in Canaan and closes (50:12–14) with its fulfillment. Adjoining each of these terminal sections is an account of mourning: seventy days in Egypt (50:1–3) and seven days in Canaan (50:10, 11). In the middle is the honorary funeral procession—Pharaoh's authorization of it (50:4–6) and the actual journey to Canaan (50:7–9).

He gave them these instructions (49:29). The whole community was associated with Joseph in his mission (cf. note on 47:29–31). On death as a gathering to one's fathers or people (49:28, 33), cf. note on 25:8. This concept reflects the biblical view of life beyond death, in contrast to Egyptian notions of immortality associated with mummification. The embalming of Jacob (50:2, 3), part of the elaborate process of Egypt's honoring him, served a utilitarian purpose in his delayed burial.

Joseph went up to bury his father (50:7). The honored home-going of the individual Israel was a testimony of faith in the coming of God's kingdom according to promise and a token of the later triumphant exodus of the nation Israel from Egypt and their victorious claiming of their heritage in Canaan. It also involved features in contrast to the Mosaic exodus, like the amiable negotiations with Pharaoh (50:4–6) and the supportive role of the Egyptian chariots and horsemen (50:9).

Joseph returned to Egypt (50:14) and his brothers to their families in Goshen (cf. 50:8), for it was not time for judgment on the lands of Ham and Canaan (cf. notes on 15:13–16).

50:15–21 ▷ The era of the three patriarchs was over. Redemptive history now became the story of the twelve tribes of Israel. A last glimpse is taken here at relationships within this covenant community in Egypt before the centuries between the close of Genesis and the age of Moses. The conflict of Joseph and his brothers (cf. 37:2–38:30) was resolved.

Joseph reminded the brothers (vv. 19, 20), still in need of reassurance of their reconciliation (50:15–18; cf. note on 45:3), that his political guardianship of the family in the foreign land was God's own providential provision (50:20; cf. 45:5, 8) for this transitional time. Thus, for the long period after his death, when they would be without patriarch or political patron, Joseph directed their trust to the almighty Lord of the covenant, their fathers' God.

50:22–26 ▷ Joseph's death, like his father's, was an act of faith (vv. 24, 25), attended by the honor of Egypt (v. 26). Like Jacob (cf. 47:28–31), he exacted from the covenant family an oath to transport his body to the promised land (cf. Exod 13:19; Josh 24:32). In so doing he voiced the redemptive hope for which the whole Genesis history had prepared: **God will surely come to you and take you up out of this land to the land he promised on oath to Abraham, Isaac and Jacob** (v. 24; cf. 48:21).

Index of Biblical References

OLD TESTAMENT

Genesis
1   34
1–3   xi
1–11   5
1–15   xviii
1:1   xviii, 9, 10, 13
1:1–2:3   3
1:2   9, 10, 13, 17, 22, 34, 38
1:2ff.   9
1:2–5   10
1:3   10
1:3–5   39
1:4   10
1:5   10, 11, 20
1:6–7   37
1:6–8   9, 11
1:8   20
1:9   11
1:9–12   39
1:9–13   11
1:12   11
1:14–18   10, 11, 39
1:14–19   12
1:16   12
1:18   12
1:20   12, 13
1:20–23   12
1:21   13
1:22   12, 39
1:24   13
1:24–25   13
1:24–27   40
1:26   12, 13, 49
1:26–28   13
1:26–31   13
1:27   13, 18, 77
1:27–28   6, 13
1:28   12, 13, 14, 19, 20
1:29   13, 20
1:29–30   11
1:30   12, 13
1:31   14, 40
2   18, 19
2:1   14, 40
2:1–3   14
2:2   11, 14, 40, 77
2:3   12, 14
2:4   17
2:4–3:24   17
2:4–4:26   17, 24
2:4–9:29   45
2:5   11, 17, 18
2:5–7   18
2:5–25   17
2:6   18
2:7   18
2:8–14   14, 18, 19
2:9   18, 19
2:14   19
2:15   19
2:15–17   18, 19
2:16–17   13
2:17   19, 20, 21, 79
2:18   20
2:18–25   18, 20
2:19–20   20
2:20   20
2:22   20
2:24   20
2:25   22
3   xviii, 17
3–8   6
3:1   21, 22
3:1–6   21, 62
3:4–5   21
3:5   43
3:6   21
3:7   22, 43
3:7–13   22
3:8   22, 24, 30, 49
3:8–13   73
3:9–13   22
3:14   22, 26
3:14–15   22, 43
3:15   xii, 22, 23, 24, 55
3:16   23
3:16–19   23, 26
3:17   23, 65
3:19   23, 30
3:20   23
3:20–21   23
3:21   24, 43
3:22   13, 19
3:22–24   24
3:23   24
3:24   13, 19, 24
4:1–2   24
4:3   25
4:3–8   25
4:4   25
4:7   23, 25, 119
4:8   25, 119
4:9   25
4:9–15   25
4:10   25

4:11 26	6:13-22 34, 40, 55	8:11 39
4:11-14 129	6:14 35, 36	8:13 39
4:14 26, 48	6:14-16 35	8:15 40
4:15 26, 27, 42	6:17 32, 34, 35, 36	8:15-17 39
4:15b 26	6:17-21 34	8:15-19 34, 39
4:16 48	6:18 36, 38, 70	8:17 40
4:17 26	6:18-21 35	8:18 40
4:17-22 26	6:18a 36, 74	8:18-19 39
4:17-24 26, 31	6:18b 36	8:19 40
4:19 27	6:19-21 35	8:20 37, 40
4:23 27	6:22 34	8:20-22 34, 40, 41
4:24 27, 31	7:1 34, 36, 40	8:20-9:17 41
4:25 27	7:1-3 36	8:20-9:29 33
4:25-26 27, 31, 116	7:1-4 36	8:21 35, 73
4:26 27, 29, 56	7:1-5 34, 36, 73, 74	8:21-22 42, 73
5 45, 51	7:2 36	8:22 41, 42
5:1 29, 70, 134	7:4 35	9 36, 49
5:1-2 32	7:5 34, 36	9:1 41
5:1-6:8 32	7:6-9 37	9:1-7 41, 42
5:2 12, 30	7:6-12 34, 37	9:2 41
5:2-32 29, 52	7:7 36	9:2-4 41
5:3 29	7:7-9 36	9:2-6 41
5:5 30, 31	7:10-12 37	9:3 41
5:8 30, 31	7:11 35, 37	9:4 41
5:14 30	7:11-12 38	9:5-6 26, 41
5:21-24 30	7:13 36	9:6 13, 42
5:22 30, 34	7:13-16 36, 37	9:7 41
5:24 30, 34	7:13-24 34, 37	9:8-17 42
5:29 31	7:16 37	9:10 13
5:32 44	7:17 37, 38	9:11 35, 42
6:1 32	7:17ff. 37	9:12 42
6:1-2 32	7:17-20 35	9:12-17 42
6:1-4 48, 57	7:18 37	9:13 42
6:1-7 31	7:19 37	9:15 35, 42
6:1-8 31	7:19-20 37	9:16 13, 42
6:2 31	7:19-23 35	9:18 43
6:3 32, 64	7:20 37	9:18-19 43
6:4 27, 32, 36, 46	7:21-23 37	9:20-27 43
6:5 31, 32, 73	7:22 40	9:21-23 44
6:7 32	7:23 37	9:22 43
6:8 32, 34, 116	7:24 38, 39	9:23 43
6:9 30, 33, 34	8:1 36, 38, 42, 75, 104	9:24 43
6:9-10 44	8:1-14 34, 38	9:25 43, 55, 56
6:9-12 33, 34	8:2 35, 39	9:25-26 64
6:9-8:22 33	8:2-3 38	9:25-27 43, 45, 92
6:9-9:29 33	8:3-4 38	9:26 43, 55, 61
6:11 31, 73	8:4 39	9:27 44, 46, 55
6:11-12 32, 34	8:5 39	9:28-29 44
6:12-16 34	8:5ff. 39	10 35, 47
6:13 32, 34, 35, 36	8:6 35	10:1 43, 45
6:13-21 34	8:6-12 39	10:1-11:9 43, 45, 51

Index of Biblical References

10:1–25:11 45
10:2 46
10:2–5 46
10:5 46, 48
10:6 46
10:6–20 46
10:7 46
10:8 32, 46
10:8–12 46
10:10 46, 48
10:11 46
10:13 46
10:14 46
10:15 46, 82
10:15–18 47
10:16 47
10:19 47
10:20 46, 48
10:21 47, 60, 124
10:21–31 47, 51
10:24 47
10:25 47, 51
10:26–30 47
10:31 46, 48
10:32 48
11:1 48
11:1–4 48
11:1–9 45, 46, 47
11:2 48
11:2ff. 48
11:4 48, 56, 100
11:5–9 49
11:7 13, 49
11:7–8 49
11:8–9 48
11:9 49
11:10 51
11:10ff. 45, 51
11:10–15 47
11:10–26 29, 47, 51, 134
11:16–26 47
11:26 54
11:27 53, 54, 81
11:27–29 54
11:27–30 81
11:27–32 54, 64
11:27–25:11 53, 81
11:28 54, 84
11:29 82
11:30 54, 64, 92, 103
11:31 54, 84

11:32 54
12–50 5
12:1 55, 66
12:1–5 54, 66
12:1–15:20 62, 64
12:2 55, 56
12:2–3 58, 123
12:3 55, 60, 72, 97
12:4 54, 55, 65, 66, 71, 87
12:5 57
12:6 56, 58, n1
12:6–7 79
12:6–9 56, 71
12:6–13:17 56, 70
12:6–14:24 53
12:7 56, 58
12:7–8 56, 95
12:8 58, 111
12:9 56
12:10 57
12:10ff. 94
12:10–20 57
12:11–13 57, 76
12:11–20 74
12:12 57
12:15 57
12:16 57, 76
12:17 57, 76
12:18–20 57
12:19–20 76
12:28–31 58
13:1 57
13:1–4 57
13:1–17 57
13:2 57
13:3 57
13:4 58
13:5 58
13:5–13 57, 58
13:6 58
13:7 58
13:8–9 58
13:9 76
13:10 57
13:10–11 74
13:10–13 75
13:11 58
13:14 58
13:14ff. 58
13:14–17 56, 58

13:14–18 57
13:15 58
13:16 59
13:17 58
13:17–20 135
13:18 59, 79
13:18–14:4 59
13:18–14:24 59, 75
14 53, 58, 62
14:1 60
14:1–2 60
14:2 60
14:3 60, 74
14:4 59
14:4–5 60
14:5–7 60
14:5–12 60
14:8 60, 74
14:10 74
14:12 60
14:13 47, 59, 60, 78, 124
14:13–16 60
14:14 60, 108
14:15 61
14:16 60
14:17–24 61
14:18 61
14:19–20 44, 60, 61, 78
14:20 60, 61, 62, 101
14:21 60, 62
14:22 61, 62
14:23–24 61
14:24 59, 60
15 80, 109
15:1 62, 67
15:1–6 62
15:1–20 62, 79
15:2 62, 84
15:2–3 63
15:3–4 86
15:4 63
15:4–6 71
15:4–8 63
15:5 59, 63
15:6 63, 67, 110
15:7 54
15:7–8 63
15:7–20 62, 63
15:9ff. 68
15:9–11 63
15:11 63

15:12 63	17:15 67, 68, 69	19:9 73
15:13 63, 64, 117, 133	17:15–22 67, 69	19:11 73
15:13–16 63, 82, 141	17:16 66, 68, 69, 116	19:12 74
15:14 57, 64, 117	17:17 66, 69, 76	19:13 74
15:15 63	17:18 69	19:14 74
15:16 58, 64, 81, 113, 117	17:18–21 66	19:15 70, 74
15:17 63	17:19 69	19:15–29 73, 74
15:17–18 64	17:20 69, 78	19:16 74
15:17–21 81	17:21 69, 70, 71	19:19 74
15:18 64	17:22 70, 71	19:21–22 73
15:18–21 56	17:23 70, 85	19:24 74
15:19–21 47, 64	17:23–27 66, 67, 70, 74	19:24–25 74
15:20 82	17:24 67	19:25 74
16:1 64, 65, 66, 103	17:27 85	19:26 74
16:1–6 65	17:28 66	19:28 74
16:1–16 82	18–19 58	19:29 72, 75
16:2 65	18:1 49, 56, 70	19:30–38 70, 71, 73, 75
16:5 65	18:1–5 70	19:37 75
16:7 56, 65, 85	18:1–15 70	19:38 75
16:7–16 65	18:1–19:38 56, 70	20:1 75
16:9 65, 85	18:1–21:34 53	20:1ff. 78, 94
16:10 59, 66	18:2 13, 71, 73	20:1–18 75
16:10–12 78	18:3 71	20:1–21:34 75
16:11 66	18:3ff. 73	20:2 76
16:12 66	18:10–14 76, 77	20:3 76
16:13 65, 66	18:12 69, 71, 76	20:4 76
16:15 66	18:14 71	20:4ff. 76
16:16 65, 66	18:15 71	20:6ff. 78
17:1 56, 66, 67, 68, 71, 131	18:16–33 71	20:7 71, 76
17:1–2 66, 67	18:16–19:29 70	20:11 76
17:1–8 99	18:17 71, 76	20:13 76
17:1–37 66	18:17–21 72	20:14–16 76
17:1–22:19 64	18:18 72	20:15 76
17:2 67	18:19 55, 72	20:17 76
17:3–8 67	18:20 72	20:17–18 75, 76
17:4 66, 67	18:20–21 73	21:1 77
17:4–6 67	18:21 13, 49	21:1–2 75, 76
17:5 68, 69	18:22 73	21:1–7 75, 77
17:6 6, 68, 114, 116	18:22–32 72	21:1–21 78
17:6–8 139	18:23 72	21:2 77
17:7 71, 101	18:23ff. 76	21:4 75, 77
17:7–8 67, 68	18:23–32 75	21:6 77
17:8 58, 67, 114	18:25 72, 75	21:6–7 76
17:9 66, 71	18:33 65, 73	21:8ff. 66
17:9–14 67, 68, 70	19:1 49, 73, 85	21:8–21 75, 77
17:10 67	19:1ff. 71	21:9 77
17:11 67, 68, 77, 112	19:1–14 73	21:10 77
17:12–13 85	19:1–38 73	21:11 78
17:13 67	19:2ff. 73	21:12 77, 79
17:14 68	19:4 73	21:13 66, 78
	19:8 74	21:13ff. 89

Index of Biblical References

21:14 78	23:17–18 83	25:19ff. 89, 92
21:18 78	23:20 83	25:19–26 92
21:20 94	24:1 83	25:19–34 91
21:21 78	24:1–9 83	25:19–27:40 91
21:22 78, 82, 94	24:1–67 81	25:19–35:29 81, 91
21:22ff. 95	24:2 83, 137	25:21 92, 103
21:22–23 78	24:3–4 84, 96, 99, 112, 121	25:22 92, 115
21:22–34 58, 75, 78	24:4 85	25:23 43, 92, 96, 110
21:23–24 78	24:6 84	25:26 92, 97
21:25–26 79	24:7 84, 85	25:27 93
21:27 78	24:9 83	25:27–34 93
21:27–30 78	24:10 84	25:28 96
21:28–29 79	24:10ff. 84, 101	25:29ff. 95, 102
21:30 78	24:10–27 84	25:30 115
21:31 78	24:14 84, 85	25:31 93
21:33 79	24:15 85	25:33 96
21:34 75, 79	24:22 85	25:34 93, 96
22 110	24:24 85	26:1 93, 95
22:1 55, 79, 80, 81	24:26 86	26:1ff. 79
22:1ff. 78	24:27 85, 87	26:1–6 93
22:1–19 79	24:28 86	26:1–33 92, 93
22:2 79, 80	24:28–61 86	26:2 56, 93
22:6 80	24:29 86	26:2–3 95
22:8 80	24:30 86	26:2–5 93, 94, 95
22:9 80	24:31 86	26:3 94, 99
22:10 80	24:36 86	26:3–4 94
22:11 80, 85	24:47 85	26:4 55
22:13 55, 80	24:48 85, 86	26:5 55, 81, 94
22:14a 80	24:50 86	26:7 94
22:14b 80	24:52 86	26:7–11 93, 94
22:15 81, 85	24:55ff. 86	26:8 94
22:17 86	24:56 86	26:12 95
22:17–18 81	24:60 86	26:12–22 93, 95
22:18 55, 81, 94	24:62–66 86, 91	26:13–14 95
22:20 82	25:1 86, 89	26:15 95
22:20–24 81, 85	25:1–6 81	26:16 95
22:20–25:11 111	25:1–11 83, 86	26:18 95
22:23 82	25:2 120	26:19–21 95
22:33 95	25:5 87	26:22 95, 96
22:50–25:11 54	25:6 86, 87	26:23–24 93
23:1ff. 81	25:7 87	26:23–33 95
23:1–2 82	25:7ff. 81	26:24 56, 94, 95, 99
23:1–20 82	25:7–11 81	26:25 79, 95
23:3 82	25:8 87, 140	26:26ff. 95
23:3–20 82	25:9 83	26:26–33 93
23:4 82, 87	25:11 87	26:28 94, 95, 96
23:6 60, 78, 82	25:12–18 66, 89, 115	26:31 96
23:9 82, 83	25:13–18 78	26:32 96
23:10 82	25:16 69, 89	26:34 96, 99, 115
23:11 83	25:19 91, 111	26:34ff. 92
23:16 82		26:34–35 96

26:34–27:40 96
27:1ff. 93
27:1–2 53
27:1–29 96
27:4 96
27:5ff. 95
27:8ff. 102
27:10 97
27:11ff. 97
27:15 123
27:15–16 120
27:20 97
27:23 97
27:24 97
27:25 97
27:26 97, 99
27:27 97
27:27–28 97
27:27–29 99
27:29 110
27:29a 97
27:29b 97
27:30–40 96, 97
27:33 97
27:36 96, 97
27:37 97, 98
27:39–40 98, 115
27:41ff. 95
27:41–28:9 98
27:41–33:17 91, 110
27:43 84
27:44–45 104
27:45 99
28:1 99, 112
28:2 104
28:3–4 114
28:4 97, 99
28:5 99
28:9 99, 111
28:10 84
28:10–22 98, 100, 107
28:12 85, 100, 108
28:13 100, 109
28:13–14 100, 114, 138
28:14 55, 59, 108
28:15 94, 100, 101, 105, 108, 113
28:17 100
28:18 100
28:20 101
28:21 101, 111

28:21–22 107
28:22 101, 113
29–31 84
29:1 101
29:1–19 101
29:1–30 101, 104
29:1–31:55 98
29:2–11 101
29:10 101
29:12–13 101
29:14 101
29:15 102
29:16–19 102
29:17–20 103
29:20 102
29:20–30 102
29:24 102
29:25 102
29:26 102
29:27 102
29:29 102
29:30 102
29:31 92, 103
29:31–35 102
29:31–30:24 101, 102
29:32–35 103
29:35 103
30:1 103
30:1–13 103
30:2 103
30:3 103, 138
30:9 103
30:14–16 103
30:14–24 103
30:16–20 103
30:17 104
30:17ff. 103
30:18 104
30:20 104
30:21 103, 112
30:22 104
30:22–23 104
30:25 104
30:25–43 104
30:25–31:55 101, 104
30:27 123
30:27–30 104
30:31–34 105
30:37–42 105
30:43 105
31:1–2 105

31:1–3 105
31:1–21 105
31:1–55 104, 105
31:3 105, 108
31:4–16 105
31:5 106
31:6 106
31:6f. 102
31:7 106
31:8 106
31:9 106
31:9–12 105
31:10 108
31:10ff. 106
31:11 85
31:13 105, 106, 113
31:14–16 106
31:17 105
31:17–21 105
31:19 106, 113
31:21 106
31:22 106
31:22–23 105, 106
31:22–24 106
31:22–55 106
31:23–42 105
31:24 105, 106
31:25–42 106
31:30 106
31:31–35 106
31:32 131
31:36–42 107
31:38 106
31:38ff. 102
31:41 106
31:42 107, 109
31:43 104, 107
31:43–55 105, 106
31:44 107
31:45–54 107
31:46 107
31:52 107
31:54 107
32:1 85, 108
32:1ff. 113
32:1–2 107, 108, 109
32:1–32 98, 107
32:2 108
32:3 115
32:3–8 108
32:3–21 108

Index of Biblical References

32:6   108
32:7   108
32:7–8   108
32:9   108
32:9–12   108, 109
32:10   108
32:11   108, 109
32:11f.   108
32:12   59, 108
32:13ff.   131
32:13–21   108
32:20   110
32:22–32   107, 109
32:24   109
32:24–30   65
32:25   109
32:25–26   109
32:28   110, 114
32:29   110
32:30   110
33:1–17   98, 110
33:3   110
33:6–7   110
33:10   110
33:11   111
33:16   111, 115
33:17   111
33:18   111, 113
33:18–20   111
33:18–35:29   91
33:19   111
33:20   111
34:1   112
34:1ff.   103, 111
34:1–31   112
34:2   112
34:3ff.   112
34:9   112
34:9ff.   112
34:13   112
34:15   112
34:16   112
34:21–24   112
34:22   112
34:25   112
34:25ff.   139
34:25–26   112
34:29   112
34:30   113, 114, 119
35:1   113
35:1–15   113

35:2   106, 113
35:3   113
35:4   113
35:5   113
35:7   101, 111, 114
35:9   56, 114
35:10   114
35:10–26   134
35:11   68
35:11–12   138
35:14   101
35:14–15   114
35:16–29   114
35:18   114
35:22   114, 118, 139
35:23–26   115
35:28   96
35:28–29   91
35:29   114, 116
36:1   115
36:1–37:1   115
36:2–3   115
36:2–5   115, 116
36:6–8   115
36:6–43   115
36:9   115
36:10–14   115, 116
36:15–19   115
36:20   116
36:20–28   116
36:29–30   116
36:31   75, 116
36:31–39   116
36:40–43   116
37   120
37:1   116
37:1ff.   114
37:2   112, 117, 122, 132, 134, 137
37:2ff.   133
37:2–4   138
37:2–9   119
37:2–11   118
37:2–36   118
37:2–38:30   117, 118, 137, 141
37:2–50:26   117, 137
37:3   118, 127
37:3ff.   138
37:5   118, 119
37:5–10   124

37:8   119
37:9   118
37:10ff.   123
37:11   119
37:12–18   119
37:12–36   119
37:20   119
37:21ff.   130
37:21–22   119, 120
37:23–25a   119
37:25   120
37:26–27   120, 130
37:28   120, 129
37:31–35   120
37:36   120, 121
38   xii, 121, 127
38:1   120
38:1–11   120
38:1–30   120, 123
38:2   121
38:6ff.   121
38:7   121
38:8   121
38:9   121
38:10   121
38:11   121
38:12–30   121
38:14   121
38:14ff.   121
38:18   121
38:21   121
38:24   121
38:26   122
38:29   122
39–41   122, 127
39–Exod 10   124
39:1   120, 121, 133
39:1ff.   120
39:1–6a   123
39:1–41:57   117, 134, 135
39:2   123
39:3   123
39:3–6   123
39:4   34
39:5   123
39:6b–23   123
39:8–10   123
39:9   123, 124
39:12   123
39:13–18   123
39:14   124

39:17 124	42:1–45:28 118, 129, 133	43:34 131
39:20 124	42:4 129	44:1ff. 131
39:21 124	42:5 129	44:1–45:15 131
39:22–23 124	42:6 129	44:9 131
40:1–4 124, 125	42:6ff. 127	44:10 132
40:1–8a 124	42:6–24 128, 129	44:12 131
40:2 124	42:7–12 129	44:14 129, 131
40:3–4 124	42:9 129	44:15 131, 132
40:8 124, 125	42:10ff. 129	44:16 131, 132
40:8b 124, 126	42:13 129	44:17 132
40:8b–23 124	42:15 129	44:18 132
40:13 125	42:15–16 128, 129, 131	44:19f. 129
40:14 125	42:16 129	44:33 132
40:15 125	42:17 130	45:1–2 132
40:18 125	42:18 130	45:1–15 118
40:20 125	42:19 130	45:3 132, 141
40:20–22 125	42:21 119, 130, 132	45:5 132, 141
40:23 125, 136	42:21–22 130	45:6–7 132
41:1 125	42:22 130	45:7 118, 133
41:1–36 125	42:23 129	45:8 141
41:8 125	42:24 130	45:10 132
41:9 125	42:25–28 130	45:10–11 135
41:9–13 125	42:25–43:14 128, 130	45:16–20 133
41:14 125	42:28 130, 132	45:16–28 128, 133
41:16 124, 126	42:29–38 130	45:21–24 133
41:17–24 126	42:32 130	45:22 133
41:21 126	42:36 130	45:24 133
41:24 126	42:37 130	45:26 133
41:25 124, 126	42:38 130	45:28 133
41:25–32 126	43–44 118	46–47 122
41:28 124, 126	43:1–2 130	46:1 79, 134
41:32 118, 124, 125, 126	43:1–14 130	46:1–4 133, 134
41:33 126	43:7 129	46:1–47:27 117, 137
41:33–36 126	43:8 130	46:2–4 134
41:37–38 126	43:8–9 132	46:3 134, 136
41:37–45 126	43:9 130	46:4 134
41:38–39 126	43:11–13 131	46:5–27 133, 134, 136
41:39 126	43:14 131	46:8 134
41:41 126	43:15–25 131	46:8ff. 7, 115
41:42 123, 127	43:15–45:15 128, 131	46:21 135
41:45 127	43:16 131	46:26 134
41:46–49 127	43:18ff. 131	46:27 45, 134
41:46–57 127, 134, 136	43:23 131	46:28 135
41:50–52 127	43:24–25 131	46:28–47:12 134, 135
41:51–52 128	43:26 129	46:29 135
41:53–57 127	43:26–28 131	46:30 135
41:54–57 123	43:26–34 131	46:31–34 133
41:57 128	43:28 129	46:31–47:6 135
42:1ff. 126	43:29 131	47:7 135
42:1–2 129	43:32 124	47:7–10 134
42:1–5 128	43:33 131	47:9 135

Index of Biblical References

47:10   135
47:11–12   135
47:13–15   136
47:13–26   134
47:13–27   136
47:14–26   136
47:21–22   137
47:25   136
47:27   134, 136
47:28–31   136, 137, 141
47:28–50:26   117, 140
47:29   137, 138
47:29–31   140
47:30   137
47:31b   137
48   137
48–49   138
48:1–2   138
48:1–22   138
48:1–49:28   137
48:3   56, 138
48:3–4   114, 138
48:4   58
48:5   138
48:5–7   138
48:6   138
48:7   138
48:8ff.   118, 127
48:8–12   138
48:10   138
48:12   138
48:13–20   97, 138
48:15   138
48:15–16   139, 140
48:16   85, 138
48:19   139
48:20   138
48:21   142
48:21–22   139
48:22   139
49   139
49:1   139
49:1–28   137, 138, 139
49:3–4   139
49:3–7   114
49:3–15   139
49:5–7   113, 139
49:8   139
49:8–12   114, 118
49:10   6, 68, 97, 110, 116, 139, 140

49:11a   140
49:11b   140
49:13ff.   140
49:16–21   139
49:18   140
49:22–26   140
49:22–27   139
49:24–25   140
49:28   140
49:29   140
49:29–32   137
49:29–33   140
49:29–50:14   137, 140
49:31   83, 138
49:33   87, 140
50:1–3   140
50:1–13   87
50:2–3   141
50:4–6   140, 141
50:7   141
50:7–9   140
50:8   141
50:9   141
50:10–11   140
50:12–14   140
50:13   83
50:14   141
50:15   132
50:15–18   141
50:15–21   137, 141
50:19–20   141
50:20   132, 141
50:22–26   136, 137, 141
50:23   138
50:24   142
50:24–25   141
50:26   141

Exodus
1:1ff.   7
1:1–7   134
1:5   45
1:5–6   134
1:8   136
1:9   95
1:9–10   105
1:11ff.   106
2:24   38
3:5   65
3:12   105
6:3   67

6:14ff.   7, 134
10:26   106
11:2   106
12:12   107
12:32   135
12:36   57
12:37–38   106
13:17   85
13:19   142
13:21   85
13:21f.   106
14:5ff.   106
14:19f.   106
15:13   85
20:3–5   113
20:11   14
21:2ff.   104
21:6   31
23:21   65
23:23   47, 113
23:27   113
23:32   60
30:25–29   100
31:13   67
31:16–17   67
32:13   38
32:34   85

Leviticus
1:3–9   80
9:24   25
19:23–25   68
20:14   121
21:9   121

Numbers
3:1   17
15:31   93
21:24   109
23:10   59
24:3–9   97
26   135

Deuteronomy
2:12   116
7:1   47
9:3   43
10:22   134
13:6ff.   21
17:14–20   116
22:20ff.   121

25:5ff. 121	3:28 19	66:10 128
26:5–8 105	4:20 59	72:8–11 140
32:4 140		73:24 31
32:10 10	**2 Kings**	76:2 61
32:11 10	6:17 108	77:20 85
32:12 85		78:14 85
32:50 87	**1 Chronicles**	78:53 85
33:1ff. 139	1:32 86	78:72 85
33:26–29 97	1:35–54 115	82:6 31
33:28 97	2 6	104:19–23 12
33:29 62	3 6	104:20–23 11
34:1–4 58	4–6 135	105:1–6 122
34:9 99	5:1 6	105:7–11 122
	5:1f. 118	105:12–15 122
Joshua	5:1–2 118	105:14–15 57
3:10 47	9:1 6	105:15 71
5:13f. 109	11:4 47	105:16 122
5:15 65	29:17 128	105:16–17 128
18:4 58		105:16–22 122
24:2 55, 84	**2 Chronicles**	105:17 122
24:3 58	1:9 59	105:17–22 122
24:14 84	3:1 80	105:21–22 126
24:24 113		105:23 117
24:32 142	**Nehemiah**	105:23ff. 122
	9:6 14, 54	105:26ff. 117, 122
Judges	9:7 54, 68	110:4 61
4:23 43	9:8 62, 63, 64	136:7–9 12
6:21 25	9:12 85	139:23 128
8:24 120	9:19 85	148:5 10
13:3ff. 71	9:19–20 10	
19:10 47	9:24 43	**Proverbs**
		8:22–23 9
Ruth	**Job**	8:28 11
3:9 24	1:7 30	8:30 35
4:5–6 121	22:14 30	8:30ff. 10, 14
4:18–22 122	28 11	
	28:38 11	**Isaiah**
1 Samuel	38 11	1:9 72
1:6 65	38:8–11 11, 35	1:10 72
		5:7 72
2 Samuel	**Psalms**	6:8 13
7:5–16 68	8:5 13	8:12–13 41
7:13 68	17:3 128	9:6–7 139
7:16 139	23:3 85	11:10 140
14:17 19	33:6 10	11:11 46
22:3 62	33:9 10	16:20 38
24:16–17 80	37:3–4 94	24:15 46
	37:18–19 94	25:8 38
1 Kings	49:15 31	26:20 40
3:9 19	51:4 123	26:21 26
		40:21 9

Index of Biblical References

40:28   9
42:4   46
43:1–6   134
43:10   9
45:18   10
49:1   46
51:1–2   58
51:2   77
51:3   19
51:5   46
53:4   109
53:12   23
54:1ff.   92
63:11–14   10
66:1   10, 14

Jeremiah
4:4   68
6:27   128
11:20   128
12:1ff.   72
15:1   71
17:10   128
23:14   72
23:16–22   71
27:18   71
34:18–20   63

Lamentations
4:6   72

Ezekiel
21:27   140
28:13   19
28:13ff.   19
31:8ff.   19
37:1–10   18
37:14   18
38–39   46
47:1   19

Daniel
1:2   46
1:17–20   125
2:1ff.   125
2:38   35
4:5ff.   125
4:22   35
5:5ff.   125
5:19   35
7:27   97

Hosea
12:3   109
12:3–4   93
12:4   109
12:4–5   114
12:12–13   105

Micah
5:6   46

Haggai
2:5   10

Zechariah
1:11   30
5:11   46
9:9   140
9:9–10   140
9:11   140

Malachi
1:2–3   93
1:6   41

NEW TESTAMENT

Matthew
1   29
1:1   6, 29, 140
1:3   122
3:12   36
5:43–48   126
10:2–4   114
10:4   114
19:26   76
23:35   26
24:31   36
24:37   33
24:37–39   37
25:10–13   38

Mark
10:27   76
10:28f.   55
10:45   80

Luke
1:32–33   140
1:48   66, 104
1:72–73   38
3:32   122
3:33   122
3:36   51
12:50   69
15:1–2   92
17:26   33
17:28–37   74
18:27   76
22:25   62
24:46   23

John
1:1   9
1:3   10
1:45   7
1:47–51   100
1:48–51   71
2:19–21   100
5:28–29   40
5:46f.   7
8:33–34   22
8:37   25
8:44   25
10:7   100
10:9   100
11:43   40
12:25   55
20:22   18
20:29   85

Acts
2:23   118
4:12   37
4:28   118
6:10   124
7:2   54
7:2ff.   54
7:4   54
7:9–10   123
7:10   124
7:14   134
10:11–15   41
13:47   46
14:27   44

Romans
1:19ff.   126
1:26–32   73
4:11   67, 69

4:13 59
4:16 63
4:16–17 67
4:16–18 59
4:17–21 63
4:19 71
4:21 71
4:22–25 63, 71
5:12–14 30
5:12–19 21
5:19 81
6:3–5 69
8:20ff. 23
9:7 77
9:8–9 66
9:10–13 92
9:12–13 43, 92
9:14–16 92
9:29 72
11:16 70
11:36 15
13:1–4 42
16:20 22

1 Corinthians
1:27–29 92, 113
7:14 70
11:3 20
11:7 20
11:8 20
11:9 20
15:24–28 40
15:42–49 19
15:49ff. 13
15:54 38
16:8 44

Galatians
3:6–14 63
3:7 86
3:8–9 86
3:10 13
3:16 55
3:29 59, 67, 86
4:21–27 65
4:28f. 77
4:29–30 66
4:31 66

Ephesians
4:24 13

Colossians
1:17 9
1:22 80
2:11 69, 80
2:12 69

1 Thessalonians
1:9 55

2 Thessalonians
2:1 36

1 Timothy
4:3–5 13

Hebrews
1:14 100
4:3–10 14
6:13–18 81
6:18 64
6:20ff. 61
7:4–10 61
7:7 135
7:11–8:13 61
9:1–10:18 61
11 137
11:3 10
11:4 25
11:5 30
11:7 34, 38
11:9–16 135
11:10 35, 55, 87
11:11 71
11:11–12 63, 71
11:13–16 87, 137
11:16 55
11:19 79
11:20 97
11:21 137
11:22 137
11:39 137
12:16–17 93
12:17 98
12:24 26
13:2 71, 73

1 Peter
1:11 23
2:13–14 42
3:19–20 32
3:20 38
3:21 38

2 Peter
2:5 30
2:6 74
2:6–12 73
2:7 73
2:12 13
3:3ff. 74
3:5–6 32
3:5–7 3, 33, 35
3:7 40
3:13 40

1 John
3:8ff. 22
3:12 25

Jude
7 72
14–15 30

Revelation
1:17 80
6:10 26
7:9 59
7:14 140
12 22
12:1–5 127
12:9 21
12:10–11 23
14:13 38
14:14–16 36
16:12–14 61
19:13 140
20:4–6 38
20:7–10 61
20:8 46
20:10 74
21:7 40
21:12–14 114
21:22 100
21:27 24
22:1–2 19
22:14 19

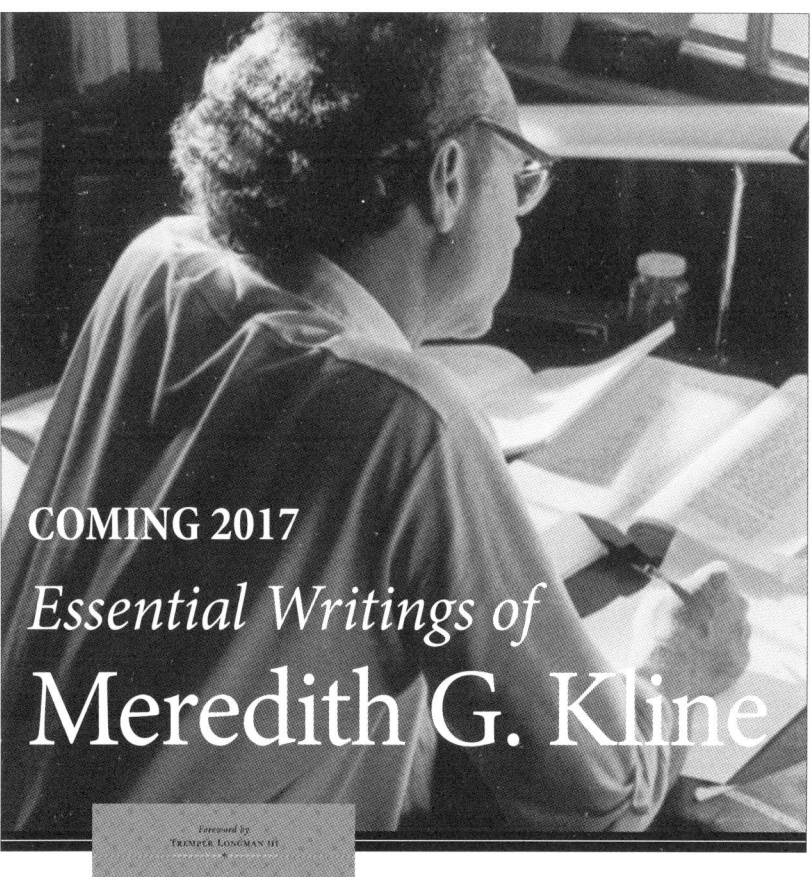

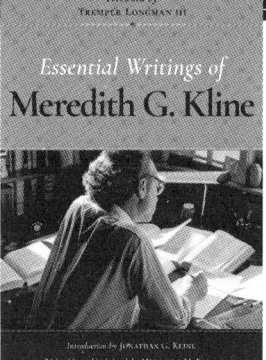

COMING 2017
Essential Writings of Meredith G. Kline

Foreword by
Tremper Longman III
Introduction by
Jonathan G. Kline
With a biographical sketch by
Meredith M. Kline

HENDRICKSON PUBLISHERS